ORIGINAL
MG T SERIES

ORIGINAL
MG T SERIES

Anders Ditlev Clausager

Photography by Tim Andrew · Edited by Mark Hughes

BAY VIEW BOOKS

Published 1989 by
Bay View Books Ltd
13A Bridgeland Street
Bideford
Devon EX39 2QE
Reprinted 1991, 1992
© Copyright 1989 by
Bay View Books Ltd

Designed by Gerrard Lindley
Typeset by Lens Typesetting
Bideford

ISBN 1 870979 06 0
Printed in Hong Kong

Contents

Introduction

The best thing about having written this book is that it has taught me a great deal more about the MG T Series! Over the years, I have learned the hard way that one treads very warily in matters regarding almost any aspect of the T Series. One is dogmatic at one's peril. Luckily there are many extremely knowledgeable people who are happy to help by pointing out the errors of one's ways – in the nicest possible way of course! Few cars seem capable of arousing so much enthusiasm and emotion as MGs of any sort, and a tremendous amount of research has been carried out as a labour of love by the many enthusiasts devoted to these cars.

What MG enthusiasm is all about was never brought home to me more clearly than in 1988 when I had the great good fortune to attend one of the Gatherings of the Faithful, held twice a year by the New England MG T Register in the USA. They invited me, or rather they invited the first MG sports car, 'Old Number One', from 1925, and were decent enough to ask me along for the ride. I met many different types of people, all united in their common enthusiasm for MGs in general and the T Series in particular, and to a man (or woman) fanatical in their dedication to pursue the most detailed minutiae concerning the originality of their cars. If I am to dedicate this book to anyone, let it be to the members of The New England MG T Register.

With so much knowledge and enthusiasm all around, writing this book has been a daunting task. The idea was to take photographs in great detail of T Series cars of all models. This was entrusted to Tim Andrew, and the result of his labours has delighted everyone connected with the project, as I am sure it will delight you as you read through the book. Tim's work is a nicely-blended mixture of beautifully composed overall shots, capturing the spirit of the lovely cars that he studied, and record shots showing in painstaking detail the smallest aspect of the individual models.

We must admit, of course, that there is a danger in relying on modern photographs as a guide to originality. No car that exists now is totally original. It has therefore been part of the task, in consultation with T Series experts, to point out where the cars photographed for this book deviate slightly from what it is now generally agreed would have been their original specification. Many such deviations concern areas where cars are

now better finished than they were originally! There are those who will argue that the only guide to originality is the archive of contemporary factory photographs. But these photos are only black and white, and therefore lack so much information which is now considered vital. It may also be pointed out that the study of contemporary photos has led eminent historians and writers into supposing that all TA two-seaters should have trafficators, or to confusing TAs and TBs. Many cars photographed by the factory at the time were prototypes or specials, and MG themselves were not above shuffling the pack and passing off a TA as a TB, or even a TC!

While Tim was out and about taking photographs, I plodded on with the text. I was fortunate to have access to original MG records, many of which I am privileged enough to look after in my capacity as archivist to the British Motor Industry Heritage Trust, others which are found in the archive of the MG Car Club. To both organisations I offer grateful thanks for their co-operation. A detailed study of the original specification books and production records for the various models has finally answered such difficult questions as how many TD Mark IIs were made, and when did the TC dashboard change from walnut veneer to Rexine? You will find the answers, and much other trivia to delight collectors of useless information, in this book.

I have also consulted published material, such as the technical and sales literature produced by the MG company when the cars were new, contemporary articles, many of the books published about them in later years (and here I must single out 'The T-Series Handbook', produced by The New England MG T Register, which has been an immensely valuable source), as well as articles often published in the various MG club magazines.

With everything gradually coming together, a draft typescript was circulated to owners of cars which had been photographed, and many owners and other experts on the T Series gathered for a seminar with Mark Hughes and myself. Going through the photos and typescript here saved me from committing to print a number of mistakes. The owners who generously allowed their cars to be photographed were: David Sambell and David Cairns (TA); Brian Hearn (the black TA and the green TF); Simon Gibbard (TA Tickford); Jeremy Targett (TB); Elizabeth Wigg (TC); Andrew Nairne (TD); and Peter Best (the prototype TF). The Arnolt-MG is one of the two owned by John Shute, Chairman of International Automotive Design, which is based in Worthing, Sussex. Our thanks go to him and to Pete Fisher, the IAD photographer, for the picture. In addition the following read the typescript or attended the seminar, or both: Ken Drake (MG Car Club T Register concours secretary); Mike Ellman-Brown (a great authority on all MGs); Ian Lloyd (MG Car Club TA to TC registrar); and David Saunders (MG Car Club T Register Yearbook editor). Several friends in the USA were also kind enough to read the typescript and give me the invaluable benefit of their comments, including Frank Cangiano, Hugh Griffin, Dick Knudson and Dave Raymond.

For special mention I must single out Ian Lloyd, who was the man who pointed us in the direction of the various cars which were photographed; and Andrew Nairne and his family who patiently and with unflagging hospitality allowed me to clamber in, over and under their TD in the course of one very long Sunday session.

To all of these great enthusiasts who were involved in the making of this book, I offer humble thanks for the inestimable help and advice which you offered. Even if at times there were differences of opinion over smaller points of originality, they were usually amicably resolved. At least we did not come to blows – or did we just agree to disagree?

Finally, I should like to thank Charles Herridge and Mark Hughes for asking me to write the book in the first place. Charles is the enthusiast's publisher who takes the classic car movement very seriously on a personal basis, and he is therefore eminently fitted to have launched this series of books. To our amusement we discovered that we share a particular passion (or perversion?) – we both own Bradfords. Mark is an old friend from the days when he as magazine editor commissioned me to write articles, and his

guidance and help in compiling this book were unstintingly given.

Both Charles and Mark know that I went to write this book with some uncertainty – I was concerned whether I could do the subject justice. In the end, I enjoyed doing it. I still do not consider myself to be an expert on the T Series and the responsibility for any mistakes in the book is mine alone. But I hope it will serve its purpose, as a vade-mecum (except it is not pocket-sized!) for the T-type student, enthusiast or owner, who is concerned not only with the originality of these cars but also with the pleasure derived from using them.

Anders Ditlev Clausager
Birmingham, February 1989

T Series Past and Present

The first of the T Series, the TA, was introduced in June 1936. Although it was not reflected in contemporary magazine articles (which as always in those days were universally favourable) it is likely that the new model was greeted by contemporary enthusiasts with some dismay. It was a somewhat larger car than previous MG Midgets, in size and engine capacity more on a par with the Magna or Magnette models. Furthermore, instead of MG's traditional overhead camshaft engine, the TA had a rather ordinary pushrod ohv engine of admittedly pedestrian parentage. In fact, the new model was a direct result of the rationalisation programme which had been instituted throughout the Nuffield group of companies (Morris, Wolseley

and MG) in 1935 by Lord Nuffield and his managing director, Leonard Lord.

Engine and transmission apart, there was still a good deal of true MG heritage in the TA. It incorporated distinct improvements such as the hydraulic brakes. It was rather more civilized and comfortable than most previous models, with useful performance – and a true top speed of 80mph. All this for only £222! Although much of the design work was carried out by the Morris drawing office at Cowley rather than at Abingdon, MG's founder and general manager (no longer managing director) Cecil Kimber still kept a watchful eye on the development of the new car, ensuring that it measured up to his exacting standard for what an MG sports car should be.

From this angle, Brian Hearn's car may be identified as a TA by the position of the bulge on the bonnet side. On the TB and TC, it was lower down.

From the front, there is little to give the game away. This car is also a TA, owned by David Sambell and David Cairns. The two-tone grey colour scheme is not an original listed colour, but the factory could produce any colours to special order.

The TA went on to become one of the most popular pre-war MG cars. Just over 3000 TAs were made over a period of three years – only the M-type MG Midget of 1929-32 had reached a higher production figure. Apart from two cars fitted with the very pretty Airline coupé body originally used on the P and N-type MGs, only the open two-seater was available until 1938, when the Tickford drophead coupé was introduced. Heavier and more expensive than the two-seater, it gave the Midget renewed appeal to customers less interested in out-and-out sports cars, and more inclined to prefer the additional degree of comfort offered by the more civilized drophead coupé body style.

On the other hand, the TA added little to MG's long list of successes in motor sport. It was never intended as a competition car, and the engine was not suitable for tuning. In the strange and somewhat parochial world of British motor sport in the 1930s, the idea of trials (or mud-plugging) had come to the fore, and factory-supported teams such as the 'Cream Crackers' and the 'Three Musketeers' used specially developed TAs to good effect.

The TB, launched in 1939 a few months before war broke out, was a TA with a much improved engine which was to prove immensely tolerant of tuning. But only 379 TBs were made before production was stopped and Abingdon was turned over to manufacture of munitions. Disagreement over war-time production led to Cecil Kimber being sacked by his boss, the managing director of the Nuffield Organisation, Miles Thomas. Then, in 1945, Kimber was killed in a railway accident. In the Abingdon factory, George Propert had taken over as general manager, and at the end of the war he had a dedicated team around him – among them Cecil Cousins, Reg Jackson, Alec Hounslow and Syd Enever (John Thornley had yet to return from war service).

Eager to get back to making sports cars as soon as possible, they got out the TB demonstrator and made a few improvements to it. With wider body, and shackles in place of sliding trunnions for the spring mounts, they launched it as the TC. By the end of 1945, 81 of the new model had been made. Abingdon never looked back from there; when the TC was discontinued in 1949, 10,000 had been

Jeremy Targett's TB sports another non-original colour scheme of silver and dark blue. Metallic grey was however available on the TB when new.

made. In the lean austerity of the post-war world, the Nuffield Organisation in common with other British car manufacturers had to export most of its output. Miles Thomas should be given credit as the man who decided to sell the MG sports car in the USA, apart from more conventional export markets.

It was the growing success of the TC in the USA which virtually dictated the design of its replacement. While the idea of a small British sports car had been accepted with alacrity by American customers, many of them would prefer left-hand drive, which was never offered on the TC. Independent front suspension would cope better with American roads, and bumpers (already fitted to North American specification TCs) were a necessity when parking in American cities. The wire wheels, although pretty, could be dispensed with in favour of more practical (and cheaper!) disc wheels. Abingdon duly complied with all these requirements and introduced the TD in January 1950. Immediately recognisable as an MG Midget, it incorporated the independent front suspension, the rack and pinion steering and some of the chassis design from the contemporary MG saloon, the 1¼-litre Y-type.

With the TD, MG became a household name in the USA. Of nearly 30,000 TDs made over a four-year period, more than 21,000 found buyers in North America. Although the TD (like the TC) was offered only as a two-seater, two variations on the theme were sponsored by American distributors. One was the lengthened four- seater made by the renowned house of Inskip in New York. The other, dealt with in more detail elsewhere in this book, was the Bertone-bodied 'family and sports car' offered by MG's Chicago distributor, Arnolt.

MG themselves offered the slightly hotted-up Mark II or TD/C model, which in production form was again mainly aimed at the American market. With this model, they extended a very careful feeler towards factory participation in motor sport. Works-prepared cars were run in sports car races by Dick Jacobs and others, and a streamlined racer was build for George Phillips to run at Le Mans in 1951. This, in turn, would sire a new generation of MG sports cars.

In fact, the production version of the Le Mans car might have been seen rather earlier than 1955 (the year of the debut of the MGA), for John Thornley and Syd Enever had a prototype ready in 1952. However, in this year the Nuffield Organisation joined forces with Austin to form the British Motor Corporation; the BMC boss was Leonard Lord, who once before had swayed MG's destiny. When Lord was shown the prototype MG he had just committed the company to build a Healey-designed sports car with an Austin engine, and did not want internal competition from a very similar-looking MG, so he turned Abingdon's proposal down.

Ultimately Lord changed his mind, but for the time being all MG was allowed to go ahead with was a slightly-modified TD, incorporating the tuned engine from the Mark II and a mild face-lift. Sympathetically received in Britain, the new TF of 1953 was ridiculed in America. MG was now competing against much more modern-looking

and powerful sports cars such as the Austin-Healey 100 and the Triumph TR2. As an interim measure, after the first year the TF was given a bored-out 1466cc engine and was dubbed the TF 1500. But it was not surprising that only 9600 TFs were made over a two-year period, before MG's new sports car generation began with the MGA in 1955.

Now, of course, the TF is as revered as any of its forebears, and if anything even more sought-after – it certainly commands higher prices than any of the earlier models. After 35 years the shape that was once described in the most unflattering terms has come into its own, and it is considered by many to be one of the prettiest MGs ever made. Indeed, all the T Series models can be described as easy on the eye, which is surely one reason for their continued and increasing popularity. Another reason is the simplicity and robustness of

The Tickford drophead coupé body was offered on both the TA and TB. This is Simon Gibbard's car which has the radiator slats painted body colour: this is correct for the Tickford.

Elizabeth Wigg's TC admirably fits the description of a 'red, rakish car' (to quote John Betjeman!).

their construction, which makes for straight-forward restoration and enjoyable running. Finally, there is that ever-lasting bit of MG Magic!

Thirty, forty or fifty years ago, when the T-types were new or nearly new, and when they were often actively campaigned, no-one thought twice about modifying the cars – especially if it would make them go faster. There was always a good market for accessories, bolt-on goodies (some of which now seem to have acquired a certain status because of rarity!) and engine tuning which was regulated by the factory in the famous 'Stage' tuning booklets. Inevitably, many T-types were treated more or less as bangers in the second-hand car market of the late 1950s and 1960s, but during the last two decades they have gained recognition as prime examples of what we now call classic cars. Many T-types are still used for racing, but generally speaking most owners are now concerned with keeping the cars in as original condition as possible for road use. The following notes have been compiled with this in mind.

left
Andrew Nairne's TD clearly demonstrates the lower and wider stance that the new chassis and smaller wheels gave this model.

below
This is also evident from the rear.

right
From the side, the family relationship with the TC is unmistakeable. An early example of the TD, this car is fitted with plain disc wheels.

below right
Yes, despite those wheels and the bumpers, we are still clearly looking at an MG Midget. The car looks its best with the hood down.

14

left
The TF is perhaps the T-type which looks best with the hood up.

below
From the rear, the differences are more subtle. Brian Hearn's TF is fitted with the optional luggage rack. Note the relative position of the tread strips on the running board and front wing. This is an example of the metallic green TF.

right
*With its flowing wing lines, the
TF is particularly rakish in the
side view.*

below
*The new front end was the major
change from TD to TF. This is
Peter Best's car, which now runs
on Michelin X radial tyres.*

KBL 296

TA, TB and TC models

CHASSIS

The TA chassis design was based on traditional MG practice. The two side members were parallel and virtually straight, except where they swept up over the front axle. At the rear the chassis went under the axle. The chassis was made from 10 gauge steel. The side members were open channel sections, partially boxed in alongside the engine. The boxed-in section continued back to just behind the third cross-member, and was extended slightly further back on the last TCs.

There was a total of five tubular cross-members, the first of which tied the dumb-irons together. The radiator was mounted on number two, and on pre-war cars this cross-member also had two brackets for canvas engine tie straps, attached via rods to the front engine plate. Just behind the second cross-member were the two front engine mounts. The third cross-member was found just behind the gearbox and supported the two rear power unit mounts. The last two cross-members supported the rear spring anchorage points. In front of the rear axle on the TA and TB models were the battery cradles for two six volt batteries connected in series (the TC had a single 12 volt battery mounted under the bonnet). Behind the axle was a shock absorber tie-bar mounted across the chassis. There were four body mounting brackets, their positions corresponding with the third and fourth cross-members. The body was also attached to the rear of the chassis, through the wooden cross-member at the bottom of the sidescreen box. The chassis and all chassis parts were finished in black.

From chassis number TA/2253, the TA and TB models had a centralised chassis lubrication system. Two groups of three nipples each were mounted on either side at the front of the scuttle under the bonnet. They served the front spring trunnion, the hand-brake cable and the rear spring trunnion on each side. This system was given up on the post-war TC model as being less necessary with the shackled springs on this model. There was undoubtedly also a cost saving, and the centralized lubrication could give trouble, unless the correct oil was used (EP 140 heavy gear oil is suitable). Separate lubrication nipples for the hand-brake cables were found on the early TAs, and were re-introduced on the TC. They were found just in front of the rear wings on each side.

Centralized chassis lubrication was found on the later TAs and the TBs. This is one of the two sets of grouped nipples.

FRONT AXLE AND SUSPENSION

The front axle beam was of I-section and was mounted above the semi-elliptic leaf springs, which were pivoted at the front. On the TA and TB, the springs ran in sliding trunnions at the back, protected by moulded rubber covers. On the TC more conventional rubber-bushed shackles replaced the sliding trunnions. The original TA front springs had five leaves and an additional two rebound leaves above the main leaf, but later cars had seven-leaf springs without rebound leaves (see the summary of modifications), as did the TB. The TC had six-leaf front springs. The TA and TB had Luvax type AR hydraulic lever arm shock absorbers, mounted ahead of the axle with their vertical movement in the fore-and-aft plane. The TC had Luvax Girling shock absorbers.

Looking under the front wing of the TC, which is correctly painted the body/wing colour – but the wing stay should also be red. Note the shroud round the lamp wiring where it disappears into the wing stay, and the coil round the brake hose. This is the correct type of shock absorber for the TC.

below
The pre-war cars such as this TB had their springs mounted in sliding trunnions at the back; the copper pipe is the feed from the lubrication nipple.

below right
On the TC, the sliding trunnions were replaced by conventional shackles.

REAR SUSPENSION

This was similar in principle to the front suspension. The semi-elliptic springs had seven leaves with two rebound leaves. They were pivoted at the front and had sliding trunnions at the rear, also replaced by conventional shackles on the TC. The shock absorbers were similar to those at the front. They were mounted behind the rear axle, with the vertical movement across the chassis frame. Some replacement rear springs are incorrectly dimensioned which results in the rear wheels sitting too far forward in relation to the rear wings.

STEERING

Conventional Bishop cam gear steering was employed, and on these three models only right-hand drive was offered. On the early TAs, the steering column was not adjustable, but in 1938 a telescopic column was introduced and this should be found on all TA Tickford coupés, and on TB and TC models. The original TA steering wheel had three solid spokes, with the rim and the greater part of the spokes covered in a black plastic material, while the inner ends of the spokes and the hub were painted silver. The hub was in two pieces held together by nine rivets, and had the MG logo in the centre.

On later TAs with the telescopic steering column, the steering wheel had a solid cast one-piece hub finished in black but with a chrome-plated cover, again with the MG logo. This type of wheel was carried over on the TB and TC models. Very many cars have been fitted with Bluemel's 'Brooklands' type steering wheel with four sprung spokes. This seems to have been a popular after-market accessory at the time and afterwards, rather than a factory-fitted item. Before the war the 'Brooklands' wheels had black rims, post-war versions had mottled grey or brown rims.

A small change on the TC gave greater clearance for the starter motor; the steering box bracket was mounted further forward on the chassis and the box was slightly higher up. Many TCs in the USA had the Bishop steering gear replaced by American-made gears which were considered more satisfactory by American owners.

The following are the correct settings for the front axle and steering: camber angle, 3°; castor angle, 6° on TA and TB; early TC, 8° (3° on beam and 5° on chassis); late TC fitted with 2½° taper plates, 5½°. Front wheel toe-in was 3/16in on the TA and TB, ¼in on the TC. The steering ratio was 8 to 1 until 1938, subsequently 11 to 1. These cars, by modern standards, had very highly-geared steering, requiring only about 1½ turns on the wheel from lock to lock.

BRAKES

The TA was the first Midget to be fitted with Lockheed hydraulic brakes, widely used on Morris and Wolseley cars since 1929, and finally fitted to an MG – the SA 2-litre saloon – in 1935. Like Ettore Bugatti, Cecil Kimber allegedly distrusted hydraulics! The ⅞in master cylinder and combined supply tank was Lockheed number 8768 on pre-war cars, Lockheed number 14923 on the TC. It was mounted under the floor inside the chassis side member and was directly activated by the brake pedal. The brake and clutch pedals rose from the floor on vertical arms through a joint moulded rubber dust excluder. The pedal pads were rectangular and slightly curved when seen from the side, and had ribbed pedal rubbers.

top
The rear springs of the TA and TB were mounted in sliding trunnions at the back; on this TB, the lubrication pipe is in evidence.

above
On the TC, the rear spring sliding trunnions were also replaced by shackles. The holes in the chassis frame are for mounting the optional luggage carrier. The exhaust tailpipe should not be polished copper!

right
Here, seen on the TA Tickford, is the original type of steering wheel – the adjustable type introduced in 1938. The hub should correctly be painted black, not silver, but the chrome-plated cover plate is correct.

below
These are the correct pedals. This TB, in common with many other cars, has lost its scuttle masking panel, so the wiring behind the dashboard is exposed. There should be an MG logo on the rubber heel mat in the carpet. The speedometer cable should correctly run in front of the toeboard and bulkhead.

The brakes worked in 9in drums front and rear, with Ferodo MT linings size 8½in by 1½in. The front brakes had 1in cylinders, the rear brakes ⅞in cylinders. The brake drums and backing plates with fittings were painted black. Some TCs had body-colour brake drums, mainly seen in contemporary pictures of show cars. In the USA, they were probably re-painted by American importers. On pre-war cars, the brake hoses were fitted with clamps, which is now not considered safe.

The hand-brake operated the rear brakes via a rotating brake cross-shaft mounted in special bearings on the chassis side members behind the gearbox. A sheathed cable ran back on each side of the car to the rear drums. The hand-brake lever was vertical, rising from the cross-shaft on the left-hand side of the gearbox tunnel in front of the gear lever, and was the usual MG fly-off type. The lever was chrome-plated and was shrouded in a black leather gaiter sewn into the carpet. The gaiter was laced at the top, to give access to a chrome-plated wing nut adjuster found at the base of the brake lever.

REAR AXLE

This was of the semi-floating type with spiral bevel final drive. The axle casing was of the one-piece 'banjo' type with a bolted-on differential casing. The rear axle ratio on the TA was 4.875:1 (8/39), but on the TB model, with its higher-revving XPAG engine, the opportunity was taken to install a lower ratio of 5.125:1 (8/41) in the interests of improving acceleration without losing out on top speed. This ratio was carried over on the TC. The rear axle was painted black.

WHEELS AND TYRES

All of these cars had wire wheels, made by Dunlop to the Rudge-Whitworth central locking pattern, with splined hubs and retained by chrome-plated two-eared knock-ons, complete with engraved MG badge. The wheels were 2.50-19 well-base rims and were always painted silver, unless the customer paid extra to have them finished in a special colour (see colour section). Special 16in wheels were available as optional extras for competition purposes.

Early TAs to chassis number TA/1769 (October 1937) had wheels laced on the outside of the rim; all subsequent cars had centre-laced wheels. Both types of wheels had 48 spokes – 16 outer and 32 inner spokes. That fashionable 1930s accessory, the Ace wheel disc (for lazy people who could not be bothered to clean their wheel spokes!) was not officially quoted an as option on the T Series but may have been fitted on some Tickford drophead coupés – as they are on the car photographed for this book.

left
This is the special medallion found on the spare wheel knock-on. When adjusted to the correct vertical position, it is pushed back in (and should then stay in place).

below
This is the type of wire wheel found on the later TAs, as well as TBs and TCs, with centre lacing. On this car it sits slightly too far forward in the wing. Also, the line of the tonneau cover when in position over the folded hood should be horizontal.

Perhaps this study of the TB spare wheel shows more clearly what is meant by centre lacing. On a side-laced wheel, the spokes were attached on the outside of the rim. The type of spare wheel carrier was common to all TA, TB and TC models. Both the carrier and its brackets are correctly painted body colour. The petrol tank strap should also be body colour, and the rear number plate backing plate seen here is a modern reproduction.

The standard tyres were Dunlop 90 4.50-19, with Dunlop Fort tyres of the same size being on the options list. The single spare wheel was mounted on a triangular body-colour bracket attached to the chassis side members and cross-member at the back of the car. Two spare wheels and a special bracket to carry them could be ordered as an option on the pre-war cars. The knock-on retaining the spare wheel had an enamel MG badge in brown and cream, of the same style as that found on the radiator. This badge was mounted on a special sprung key which ensured that it remained upright, whatever the position of the knock-on.

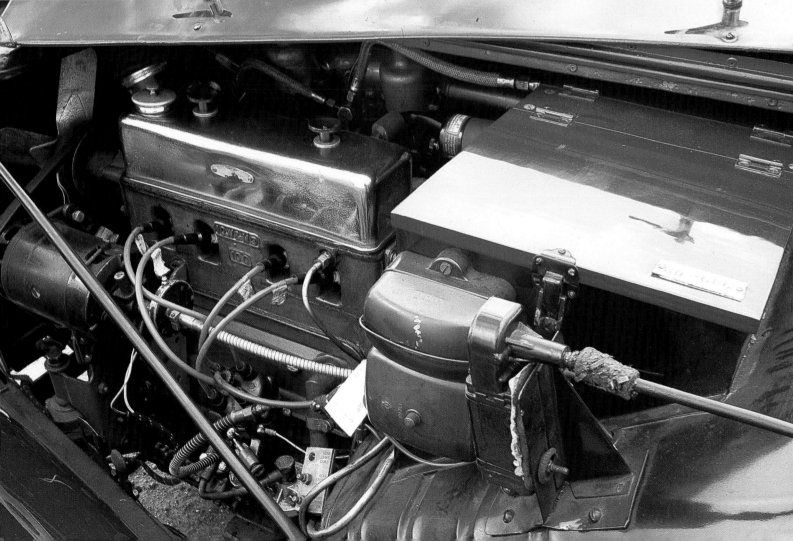

ENGINE (TA)

Here the three models can no longer be considered together, as the TA engine was of a different type to that used in the TB and TC. The TA broke with MG's tradition for using an overhead camshaft (as had the SA model) and instead had overhead valves activated by pushrods and rockers from a side-mounted camshaft. The engine was designated the MPJG type and was made by the Morris Motors Engines Branch (the old Hotchkiss company). It was based on the Wolseley 10/40 engine which in turn was an overhead valve version of the Morris Ten engine, and a similar ohv engine was subsequently used in the Morris Ten Series III of 1937-38. The stroke was 102mm, which was a very traditional dimension for Morris engines; with a bore of 63.5mm, the engine was rated at 10hp under the old RAC hp taxation formula. Capacity was 1292cc, compression ratio was 6.5:1, and power output was 50bhp at 4500rpm. For competition work, the cylinder head could be machined to increase the compression ratio to 7.3:1 (see detailed list of competition parts elsewhere in this book).

The combined cylinder block and crankcase, of cast iron, extended well below the crankshaft centre-line and was finished off with a ribbed sump made from cast aluminium. The cylinder head was of cast iron. The basic engine assembly was painted a bright red, almost orangey, colour. The crankshaft ran in three main bearings, with loose bearing caps lined with white metal; the big end bearings were also lined with white metal. The pistons were made by Aerolite and on early engines had two compression rings and two scraper rings. From engine number MPJG/697 they were replaced by simpler pistons with only one scraper ring. The camshaft ran in three bearings, it was mounted on the left-hand side of the engine and was driven by duplex chain from the crankshaft. The tappets were mounted in two separate bearing blocks. There was a single tappet inspection cover with a fume extractor. Originally the valves were fitted with double valve springs, but from engine number MPJG/1605 triple valve springs were employed. The valve diameter was 30.5mm for the inlet valves, 26mm for the exhaust valves.

The inlet ports were siamesed for the front and rear pairs of cylinders respectively. There were three exhaust ports, one each for the front and rear cylinders, and a siamesed port for cylinders number two and three. The manifolds were on the right-hand side of the engine. The rocker cover was made from chrome-plated pressed steel with the oil filler cap at the front. It was retained by two anodised metal finger nuts. Some cars (and this applies also to the later T Series models) have acquired cast aluminium 'coffin' type rocker covers, with an octagonal quick-release oil filler cap, similar to the cam covers seen on the earlier MG ohc engines. The lubrication system was the conventional wet sump type, with a total capacity of 1½ imperial gallons. The oil pump was driven from the camshaft, and there was an external Tecalemit oil filter.

The engine was the TA's Achilles'heel. While it gave the car adequate performance, the lengthy stroke inhibited the engine's potential, making it less susceptible to tuning, and there was always a danger of over-revving. Another problem area was that the cylinder block had very narrow waterways, and was prone to cracking from freezing in winter. In consequence many TAs have been fitted with the much better XPAG engine from the TB and TC models.

ENGINE (TB & TC)

In the autumn of 1938, Morris had introduced the new Series M Ten which featured an all-new power unit, the XPJM type. In basic design principles it differed little from the previous generation of Morris engines, but the important change was that the stroke had been reduced to 90mm (as on the Morris Eight). The new Morris still had a 63.5mm bore to keep it in the 10hp bracket, and therefore a capacity of 1140cc. This engine formed the basis for the new MG Midget engine which was launched, rather quietly, in the TB model in April 1939. In MG form, the bore was increased to 66.5mm, giving the TB a capacity of 1250cc. It also meant that the new Midget was rated at 11hp. The compression ratio was increased to 7.25:1 and the power output was 54.4bhp at 5200rpm. Maximum torque was 64lb ft at 2600rpm. This engine was known as the XPAG type, and in largely unmodified form (except for the addition of a timing chain tensioner) was also used in the TC model after the war.

Much of what has been said about the general architecture of the TA engine also applies to the TB/TC engine. Among the important differences was the fact that the crankshaft was now fully counter-balanced and thin steel wall shell bearings were used for the mains and the big ends. The tappets were mounted directly in the cylinder block. The cylinder head had separate inlet and exhaust ports for all cylinders. The crankcase now extended downwards only to the crankshaft centre-line. The sump was longer than on the TA, but with the adoption of a dry clutch (see the transmission section), total oil capacity was reduced to 1⅛ imperial gallons. The oil filter was of an improved design. On the TB model, two types of rocker cover were quoted – either the chrome-plated pressed steel type (with ebonite or bakelite nuts) or the cast aluminium type. Most TC engines had the pressed steel rocker cover, now painted a silver-grey-green rather than chrome-plated, but the cast aluminium type was fitted between engine numbers XPAG/2020 and XPAG/2966 in 1946-47, according to the parts list. On the TB and TC engines, the oil filler cap was at the rear of the rocker cover. With the XPAG engine came a dipstick with an MG badge on the handle.

The valves were bigger than on the TA engine, with diameters increased to 33mm (inlet) and 31mm (exhaust). The XPAG engine was

The carburettor side of the TA engine. The bulkhead is painted the correct black. This is an early TA which lacks the centralized chassis lubrication system.

This engine is fitted in the TA Tickford. The bright red engine colour shows up well, and the chrome-plated rocker cover is correct. Note the under-bonnet mounted wiper motor on this model, and the Tickford body number plate on the toolbox lid.

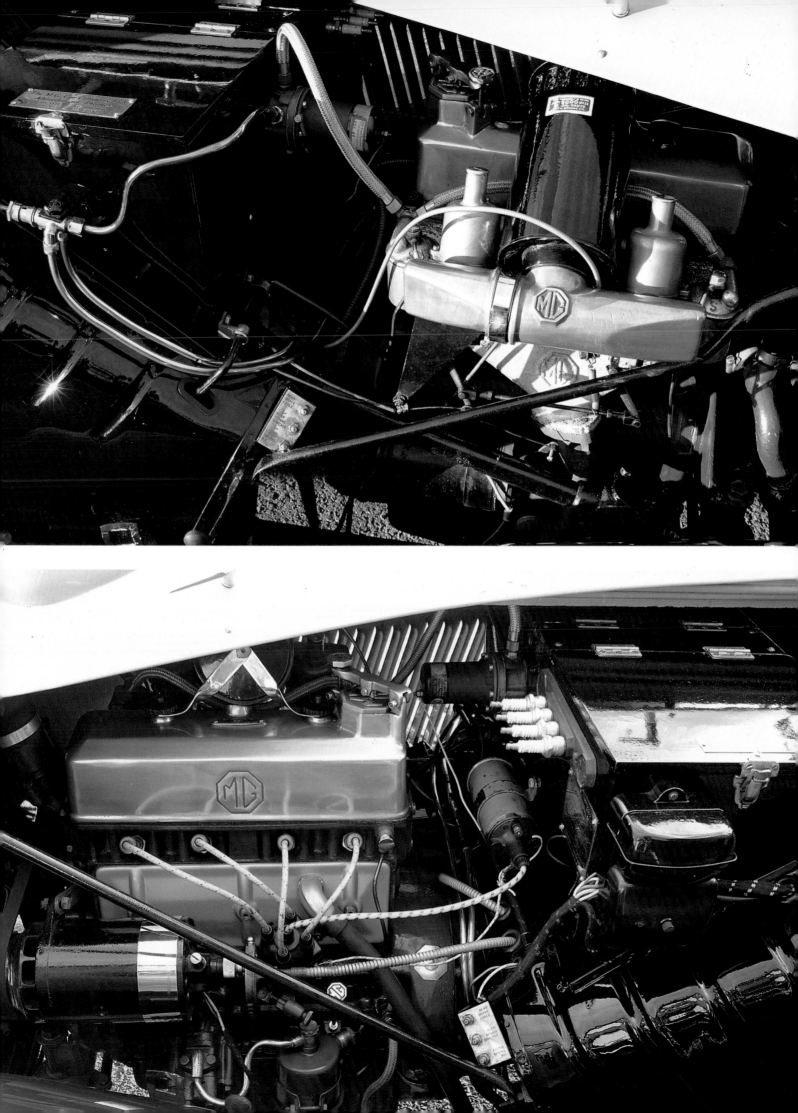

somewhat lighter than the MPJG unit, so overall weight for the TB was down ¼cwt compared to the TA. A small difference between the TB and the TC concerned the pressed steel engine-coloured tappet cover, which on the pre-war engines had a turned-in edge, lacking on post-war models. As originally fitted in the TB, the engine was painted red, but a darker, more mauve-ish shade than the TA engine. After the war, TC engines were at first light grey but it is thought that they later changed to a grey-green colour, before the red engine colour was re-introduced around chassis number TC/5000 in March 1948. However, I must admit that there is still some dissension among the experts on the correct sequence and shades of TC engine colours!

left
This engine could be in a TB or a TC, but the absence of the battery, the black bulkhead and the lubrication nipples identify it as a TB. The TB engine was a darker red colour than the TA. The cast aluminium rocker cover was one of two alternatives found on this model.

below left
On the ignition side of the TB engine, the MG octagon on the dipstick handle is just visible above the radiator stay. The tappet cover should be painted engine colour.

The octagonal engine number plate was found on the TB and TC, fixed on the left-hand side of the flywheel housing (this is a TC). This type of square-section coiled shroud for the speedometer and rev counter cables is correct for the post-war models. Pre-war cars had round-section coil.

below
The red engine and body-coloured bulkhead are correct on later TCs. All TCs had the rocker cover painted this silver-grey colour. Note the N.O.L. can of spare oil in its holder on the battery box.

The black finish is correct for the dynamo and starter motor on all models, but the ignition coil should also be black. The upside-down position of the coil is correct on the TC.

Looking at the TB again, with one of the two moulded insert trays for the toolbox. The spare plug carrier is probably the type that was offered by MG at the time, being marked 'Lodge' and 'MG' in the two octagons. The type of chassis number plate is common also to the TA but was altered slightly on post-war cars.

Brian Hearn's TA is black with red trim, and has the radiator slats painted correctly red to match the upholstery.

thermometer fitted to the radiator cap was, and remains, a popular accessory among American T-type owners.

A particular point concerns the colour of the radiator slats. These were usually painted to match the upholstery colour. On the TA and TB, upholstery usually matched the body (compare the colour section) so evidently the radiator slats were painted body colour, but contrast colour upholstery was found on cream, black and some green cars, and these would then have the radiator slats in the upholstery colour. On TCs (and, presumably, TDs), if a car was green with green upholstery, or red with red upholstery, the slats were painted body colour; but on a black or cream car with red or green upholstery, the radiator slats were finished in shades of red or green which were rather brighter than the normal MG Red or Shires Green used for the paint on the body on cars in these colours.

EXHAUST SYSTEM

With the exhaust ports from cylinders number two and three siamesed, the TA had an aluminized three-branch exhaust manifold, inevitably with the MG logo cast in. This led to a single downpipe running back on the right-hand side of the car. The downpipe incorporated a flexible section to compensate for the fact that the exhaust system was rigidly mounted to the chassis. A two-bolt flange linked the pipe to a single Burgess straight-through tubular silencer mounted to the chassis under the floorboards. There was a single tailpipe. The exhaust pipe and silencer were painted black.

On the TB and TC, which had separate exhaust ports for all cylinders, the exhaust manifold had four branches; otherwise the exhaust system was not changed.

CARBURETTORS AND FUEL SYSTEM

All the TA, TB and TC models used two SU carburettors, size 1¼in, of the semi-downdraught type (which meant that they were mounted at a slight angle). On the TA they were type HV3, with standard needles AC, while the TB and TC had H2 carburettors, with standard needles ES. The carburettors had round brass tops, with 'penny' slots. There was a single SU low-pressure (L-type) electric fuel pump mounted to the right of the front of the toolbox, or to the left of the front of the battery box on the TC. A cylindrical AC air cleaner painted black and containing oil-wetted woven steel mesh was used. On the TA it was situated at the back of the engine compartment, with a tubular air inlet manifold running forward to the carburettors. On the TB and TC, a larger air cleaner was mounted at an angle above the rocker cover, between the carburettors, and secured with a bracket to the rocker cover nuts. The air manifold was in natural aluminium on all cars, and on the TB and TC had the MG logo cast in.

COOLING SYSTEM

Previous MG Midgets had relied on simple thermo-syphon cooling, but the TA had a water pump (which was very prone to leakage) and a four-bladed fan, while the temperature was regulated by a thermostat. The radiator and header tank were black. The TA had a red fan, while the TB and TC had a black fan. The radiator cowl was chrome-plated and had an enamel MG badge on the false nosepiece, with the border and letters in brown and a cream background. The external filler cap was octagonal and chrome-plated. Although the TB had a new type of radiator core, and the top water hose from the engine outlet was central in the header tank, the cooling system remained the same in principle, and there were no further changes on the TC model. As there was no means of monitoring the coolant temperature – except for obvious distress symptoms, if the worst should happen – an external Moto-Meter

far left
This shows the petrol tap control on the dashboard, in the correct black finish with white lettering.

left
With the exception of the early TAs, this type of quick-release petrol cap is found on TA, TB and TC cars. The release lever is engraved with the word 'PRESS', whereas the TD and TF had an MG octagon. On this TC the petrol tank straps are painted correctly in body colour.

below
On the pre-war cars you would find this two-way petrol tap under the bonnet. The toolbox clip should be painted the same colour as the bulkhead.

The fuel tank was strapped to the rear chassis cross-member and to the rear of the body. The original wide TA tank (see summary of modifications) held 16 imperial gallons (approximately 72 litres) of which 3 gallons were held in reserve. The later TAs, and all TB and TC models, had a narrower tank holding 13½ gallons (61 litres) still with a reserve, on the pre-war cars, of 3 gallons (14 litres). The pre-war cars had a petrol tap on the dashboard, and had two outlet pipes at the bottom of the petrol tank, the main pipe finishing at a higher level inside the tank than the reserve pipe. On the TC the petrol tap was replaced by a warning lamp for low petrol level so there was only one outlet pipe to the tank, but a sender unit for the warning lamp was added.

The tank and its retaining straps were painted body colour. The end plates were chrome-plated but the chrome was painted over, except for the raised edges of the end plates which were left in polished chrome. The nuts retaining the end plates were chrome-plated. The fuel filler cap was on the left-hand side; it was made from chrome-plated brass and was the quick-release type. Two different types were found on the TA – the early caps had the release button on the side, later cars with the narrow tank had a filler cap with a release lever with the word 'PRESS'.

TRANSMISSION

Together with its Morris-inspired engine, the TA inherited another Morris characteristic, a cork-lined clutch running in oil which was fed through from the engine lubrication system. The clutch driven plate had 46 cork inserts and the clutch was mechanically operated. The gearbox was of a design common to several Morris, Wolseley and MG cars of the period, but initially the gearbox lacked synchromesh. This was added, on top and third gears only, from engine number MPJG/684.

The internal gearbox ratios were unique to the TA, being rather closer than on other Nuffield cars of the period. There were two different sets, for the non-synchromesh and for the synchromesh gearbox respectively. The following table lists the internal and the overall gear ratios, in conjunction with the standard final drive ratio of 4.875:1:

	Non-synchromesh box		Synchromesh box	
	Internal ratios	Overall ratios	Internal ratios	Overall ratios
First	3.715:1	18.11:1	3.454:1	16.838:1
Second	2.2:1	10.725:1	2.04:1	9.95:1
Third	1.421:1	6.928:1	1.32:1	6.435:1
Top	1.00:1	4.875:1	1.00:1	4.875:1
Reverse	4.77:1	23.26:1	4.44:1	21.645:1

The lid of the gearbox was fitted with a cast aluminium remote control extension for the gear lever, which was chrome-plated. Originally the TA had a flat, mushroom-shaped gear lever knob with an engraved gate. Later on (but it is not certain whether during the TA's or the TB's production run) this was replaced by the more usual pear-shaped knob, also found on the TC and later models. This had single lines engraved between the gear positions. The shift pattern was the normal H, with reverse to the right of top gear. At the bottom of the gear lever was a chrome-plated, domed pressed steel dust cover (with an oiling hole) which sat under the gearbox rubber cover.

There was an open, one-piece balanced Hardy-Spicer prop-shaft with two universal joints; this was painted black. The gearbox and the bell housing were finished in engine colour, but the gearbox lid and the remote control were left in natural aluminium.

A major change occurred on the TB model with the new XPAG engine. On this model, a dry Borg & Beck single plate clutch of 7¼in diameter was fitted, and the gearbox now had synchromesh also on second gear. Gearbox ratios were revised, and the TB and TC ratios were as follows (with the standard final drive of 5.125:1):

	Internal ratios	Overall ratios
First and reverse	3.38:1	17.32:1
Second	1.95:1	9.99:1
Third	1.35:1	6.92:1
Top	1.00:1	5.125:1

Apart from an improved type of clutch facing, there were no changes to the transmission on the TC, or during the production run of this model.

ELECTRICAL EQUIPMENT AND LAMPS

The electrical equipment was supplied by Lucas. The two six volt batteries on TA and TB models, mounted in cradles in front of the rear axle, were type STLW11E with lids. The TC 12 volt battery mounted on the bulkhead was type STXW9A. Battery capacity was 50 AH. The electrical system was wired positive to earth. The wiring had rubber insulation and cotton cover, black on the pre-war cars, colour-coded on the TC.

The TA and TB had a three-brush dynamo, type C45NV2. The TC dynamo was type C45YV, and the TC was fitted with a compensated voltage control regulator. The starter motor was type M418A84 on the TA and TB, and type M418G on the TC. Both the starter motor and the dynamo were painted black. The distributor on the TA was type DK4AA35, on the TB and TC type DKY4A. Both types had automatic advance and retard, and a manual micrometer adjustment. The ignition coil was type Q12/8LO, attached to the toolbox on the bulkhead (the battery box on the TC), horizontal on the TA, upside down on the later models. The plugs on the TA were Champion L.10 (14mm) with ½in reach (modern equivalent: L.874) and push-on plug caps were fitted. Champion L.10S plugs were quoted for the TB and TC. The firing order for both the MPJG and the XPAG engines was 1,3,4,2.

The cut-out and resistance on the TA and TB models was type CJR3L35. This and the fusebox containing six fuses were mounted on the left-hand end of the toolbox. The TC had a type RF91 voltage regulator, mounted on the right-hand end of the battery box. TCs had only two fuses, originally found inside the cover of the voltage regulator. From chassis number TC/3414 in August 1947, an RF95/2 voltage regulator with exposed fuses was fitted.

The headlamps were mounted on body-colour brackets between ears on the radiator cowl and the front wings. The lamps had chrome-plated shells and rims. A Lucas medallion on the lamp shell was raised above the surface on pre-war lamps, and countersunk after the war. Before the war the rim was fixed with a screw, after the war with a clip. The early TA headlamps had a flat rim; later TAs and TBs had headlamp rims which curled inwards and formed a raised lip around the glass. The glasses were slightly convex and usually had the horse-shoe (U-shaped) pattern, but some TCs had more domed headlamp glasses with the diamond or cat's eye pattern. Home market cars had headlamps type LBD 140EDS (TAs with solenoid dipping), M140 or MBD140 (TC).

On cars supplied in the home market, the now illegal 'dip-and-switch' system was used. The left-hand (nearside) lamp was dipped, and the right-hand (offside) lamp was switched off. On the TA the left-hand lamp had a dipping reflector controlled by a solenoid, while on the TB this lamp had a special bulb with a flat-topped beam, so it was permanently dipped. The TC had a double filament bulb in the left-hand lamp, and these should now be fitted to both headlamps to achieve double-dipping lamps to comply with present-day requirements. Double-dipping lamps, type LBG150 or LD140EF, were normally fitted to export cars at the time, and were optional in the home market, being recommended on cars sold 'for continental touring' (I should think so, too!).

The sidelamps were type 1130 with round (not octagonal) bodies. They were chrome-plated, with chrome-plated rims and frosted glass lenses without any lettering. The earliest TAs may have had chrome-plated Lucas medallions set in the lamp bodies, otherwise a red translucent plastic 'King of the Road' lens was fitted in the top of the lamp.

A single combined stop and tail lamp with two separate bulbs was fitted to one side of the rear number plate, and through a clear window in the side of the lamp housing it also served as number-plate illumination. On the TA it was a round, single lens lamp, type ST38, either black with a chrome-plated rim or all chrome-plated. It had a Lucas medallion and ribbed glass. From body number 1790 (towards the end of the TA run, or from the start of the TB) a D-shaped ST51 lamp was fitted. This had a vertically split two-piece glass, and a chrome-plated housing. It was also found on the TC. To comply with modern rules, cars should have two stop and tail lamps. The most tasteful way of doing this is to fit another lamp of the same type on the other side of the rear number plate.

Trafficators were quoted as an optional extra on TA and TB two-seaters and were fitted as standard on the Tickford coupe. The oft-seen photo of a TA two-seater with trafficators built into the scuttle sides is of one of the two 1936 prototypes. The TC did not have any signalling devices except on the 1948-49 North American cars (see separate section) – MG's motto might have been, "It's what your right arm is for". For reasons of safety as well as legality, it is obviously desirable to add flashing indicators on these cars now. They can be built into the front sidelamps, and small orange flashers can be discreetly added on brackets outboard of the tail lamps at the back. The alternative is to make the stop lamp bulbs do the flashing, but this is likely to confuse most drivers following behind. Rear reflectors were not fitted originally but are also a desirable addition, in the interest of safety.

On the badge bar at the front was fitted a chrome-plated fog lamp at one end, originally type FT27, changed in 1948 from TC/4739 to type SFT462. On the other end of the badge bar was an 'Altette' horn, type HF/934/2 or, on the TC, type HF1234. The diaphragm was painted crackle black, the rim was chrome-plated and the housing and bracket were black. The nuts on the pre-war horns were of a scalloped pyramid design, the TC horns had domed nuts; all were chrome-plated.

It should be noted that on cars sold in the home market and in other countries which drove on the left, the horn and the tail lamp were mounted on

The U- or horseshoe-shape pattern is common to the headlamp glasses on most TA, TB and TC cars, except some later TCs. This TB also has the turned-in headlamp rim found on the TBs and some TA cars.

On pre-war cars such as this TB, the Lucas medallion sits proud of the headlamp shell; post-war cars had the medallion countersunk into the shell.

With the possible exception of early TAs, the 'red dot' is believed to be correct on the sidelamps on all cars.

right
Most cars have tail lamps which are completely chrome-plated, but black lamps with a chrome-plated rim may be original on some TAs. The round lamp was found only on the TA. This is the correct shape for the rear number-plate backing plate, with an 'ear' for the lamp. Of course the registration mark can be painted directly on the backing plate. The reflector is a necessary modern addition, but this is a good way of mounting it.

far right
The D-shape tail lamp seems to have come in with the TB and was continued on the TC, as seen here. This is a reproduction backing plate; the original had square ends.

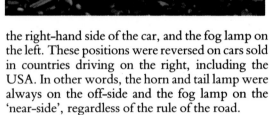

the right–hand side of the car, and the fog lamp on the left. These positions were reversed on cars sold in countries driving on the right, including the USA. In other words, the horn and tail lamp were always on the off-side and the fog lamp on the 'near-side', regardless of the rule of the road.

The two-seater had a wiper motor type CW3/4DA, or SW4 on the TC. It was painted crackle black, with a chrome-plated switch on the motor housing. It was fitted to the left on the top of the windscreen frame, in just the right spot to 'brain' a hapless passenger in an accident! There were two wipers, with chrome-plated arms and a cross bar which was kinked to clear the bonnet hinge when the screen was folded flat. The Tickford coupé had a remote wiper motor and wipers below the windscreen.

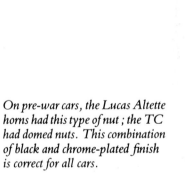

On pre-war cars, the Lucas Altette horns had this type of nut; the TC had domed nuts. This combination of black and chrome-plated finish is correct for all cars.

This is the type of fog lamp used on all cars until the TC in 1948.

BODY AND BODY TRIM

The body was constructed on classic coachbuilding principles, with an ash frame reinforced by a steel framework and incorporating some plywood panelling; it was covered in steel panels. The bodies were supplied by Morris Motors Bodies Branch in Coventry, although the front bulkhead was added by MG at Abingdon. This was the reason why the bulkhead was not originally painted in body colour. On the TA and TB it was black, on the TC it was at first light grey but a change was made to a body-coloured bulkhead in 1948. Most experts agree that the engine colour was changed to red at the same time.

Being prone to attack from rot as well as rust, the body was by far the weakest area on any T-type. Fortunately, all body parts are available, even to the extent that complete replacement body kits are manufactured.

The basis for the body ash frame were the two bottom rails under the doors; these were reinforced by the steel 'body chassis frame' members which also incorporated vertical extensions, joined to the front side pillar and the door hinge pillar at the back. The front side pillar and the front door (locking) pillar were joined at the top by cross-members to which the scuttle top panel was attached. The doors had two hinges

which were painted body colour. The hinge pillars were quite substantial, and joined the rather intricate rear wheel arch top members. A back panel completed the basic wooden frame. A detachable plywood panel nestled in a wooden frame at the bottom of the tonneau; this gave access to the rear axle and shock absorbers, and to the batteries on the TA and TB models. The floorboards were made from seven-ply plywood, in one piece on either side of the propshaft tunnel, and were originally left untreated. They were attached to the tunnel, to the front toeboard and side pillars, and with brackets to the heelboard. The propshaft tunnel was a steel pressing, painted black and fixed to the chassis crossmembers. The toeboard at the front of the bulkhead was another steel pressing, usually painted black, but on the TC may also be grey or body colour to match the bulkhead.

The external panels were mostly extremely simple, only the double-humped top scuttle panel and the wings having any pronounced curvature. Where the wings met the bodywork or valances, there was body-colour beading made from Rexine wrapped round a cord centre. The wing stays and the underside of the wings were painted body colour. The running boards were separate pressings, bolted to the front wings with a beading, and did not quite butt up to the rear wings. It is debated exactly how much of a gap

above
No-one seeing the new TA in 1936 could have doubted that this was a true MG Midget. The basic shape had been introduced with the J-type in 1932 . . .

above right
. . . although the flared wings were only added in 1933. By 1936 the shape had been refined to something close to perfection and no great change was found necessary before 1950.

right
There were detail differences between early and late TAs: the first ones had a wider petrol tank and narrower rear wings without the stiffening rib. This rear view of a later TA is typical also of the TB and TC models.

above left
The MG radiator was introduced in 1927 and the slats added in 1935; it would survive in recognisable form to the 1970s.

above
The design of hood and sidescreens was similar on all three models. When raised, the hood detracts little from the cars' looks.

right
The fold-flat windscreen was *de rigueur* on sports cars at the time. The humped scuttle supposedly offered some protection when the screen was folded. Aero screens were a desirable extra for the serious racer.

left
The TB used exactly the same body as the later TAs, so there is very little external difference between the two cars.

there should be here – about 1¼in seems to be right! At the front end of the car was a valance or apron in the area between the chassis dumb-irons, with six louvres of increasing width from front to rear forming a triangular pattern. It was secured by body-coloured bolts, which on restored cars often end up being chrome-plated.

Some confusion has arisen because MG had the infuriating habit of handing out publicity pictures of a prototype TA (registered CJO 617) well into the TA's career. This car, which on occasion has even had to pose as a TC, had only 15 bonnet louvres and trafficators built into the sides of the scuttle. In fact all production TA, TB and TC models had 21 bonnet louvres, and trafficators were not fitted on two-seaters as standard. The central bonnet hinge was made from chrome-plated brass and had chrome-plated end caps. Rubber protectors were fitted with rivets to the bottom corners of the bonnet side panels. All of these cars had a pear-shaped bulge on the left-hand bonnet side panel to clear the dynamo. On the TA it was situated about halfway up the louvres, on the TB and TC it was lower down, towards the bottom of the louvres.

Opening the bonnet revealed a bulkhead-mounted toolbox, accessible from either side with lids hinged in the centre, fastened by clips painted in the colour of the bulkhead. TA and TB toolbox lids were from nine-ply plywood. Early TAs had felt-lined toolboxes, with the small tools stored in a canvas roll. Later TAs and TBs had inserted

To the casual observer, the TC is identical to the pre-war cars, since the extra width in the body between the door hinge pillars hardly shows.

The door hinges were body colour, as was the piping between body and wings. The three tread strips to the running board were found on pre-war cars. The reflection of the running board in the rear wing clearly shows the gap between the two.

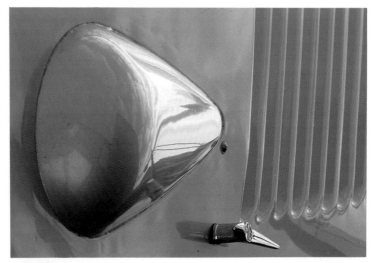

above
This pattern of the 21 bonnet louvres was common to all TA, TB and TC cars. The group of three shortened louvres towards the back allows the fitting of the rear bonnet lock.

above right
The bulge on the bonnet side affords clearance for the dynamo. As seen here on the TB (but also applicable to the TC), it lines up with the bottom of the louvres; on a TA it would be somewhat higher up. The bonnet handles are similar in design to the door handles, and should sit horizontally when locked. The screw seen above holds the actual bonnet lock in place.

right
If you compare this TA toolbox with the TB toolbox shown earlier, you will notice that this is the other moulded tray. There is some debate as to which moulded tray should be found on which side of the toolbox.

moulded rubber tool trays for the smaller tools. Below these trays the larger tools were held in place by clips. The jack was clipped to the front panel of the toolbox, and rested on a wedge-shaped block of wood. Clips on the sloping bulkhead panel held the jack handle shaft, the wheel hammer, the grease gun and the tyre pump. The TC had a lidded battery box in front of the toolbox, which was therefore considerably narrower. No tool trays were fitted, and tools were simply stored in a canvas roll. The TC toolbox was lined with cream or off-white felt, and the toolbox lids were metal. All cars were supplied with a spare can of oil, but only on the TC was there a special holder for it on the front of the battery box.

40

above
The door sill plates were originally of this neatly lettered design until plain sill plates were introduced on later TCs.

above right
You would naturally expect an MG octagon in the door handle. The escutcheon is in the shape of an elongated octagon, and this and the octagon in the door handle should be at the same angle.

right
The original type of rear-view mirror was mounted on the windscreen stanchion. Rectangular in shape, it could be adjusted for vertical or horizontal fitting. The Lucas medallion was found only on the pre-war mirrors.

Although they are nearly indistinguishable to the casual observer, there were in fact three different types of open two-seater bodies fitted to these cars. The original TA body was body type number B.269. This can be distinguished by its narrow rear wings without a central stiffening rib, and the wide petrol tank. In 1937, it was replaced by body type number B.270 with wider rear wings incorporating a central rib, and a narrower petrol tank. This body was continued on the TB. The TC had body type number B.280, the main difference being that it was 4in wider between the rear door pillars. A quick way of telling a TC from a pre-war car is by looking at the running boards: on the TA and TB they had three tread strips each, while the TC only had two. These strips were of rubber set in aluminium. The scuttle area remained the same width so the windscreen was the same on all three models, and the bonnet was the same width also.

The bright body trim parts were chrome-plated. These included the bonnet handles and the door handles which were of similar design, like an elongated diamond in shape with the MG octagon towards the front. The two bonnet handles on either side should appear horizontal – if not, the locks are worn! The door handles were aligned parallel with the sloping, cut-away part of the door top. The door handle escutcheons were vertically elongated octagons, and should be at the same angle as that of the MG badge in the handle itself. The two-seater did not have external key-operated locks.

The windscreen was made by Auster and was fitted with toughened Triplex glass (except for some export TCs which had laminated glass). A small Auster badge appeared on the inside of the bottom frame. The frame and pillars were chrome-plated. By loosening a wing nut on either side, the windscreen could be folded flat over the bonnet. A rubber apron provided a seal between the windscreen frame and the scuttle, and rubber gaskets were interposed between the pillars and the bodywork. The pillars should be flush to the curvature of the scuttle panel, and they should stop above the panel break line on the side of the scuttle.

A rear view mirror, Lucas type 160 in chrome-plated finish, was mounted on an arm on the right-hand windscreen pillar, so it could be used also when the screen was folded flat. The mirror was rectangular in shape and could be turned for vertical or horizontal position. Pre-war mirrors had a Lucas medallion which was discontinued on the post-war version. A chrome-plated badge bar was fitted above the front dumb-iron apron. In addition to the horn and fog lamp previously mentioned, it carried a centrally mounted bracket for the starting handle.

Black-painted backing plates for front and rear number plates were fitted to all home market cars, but that on the front was deleted on some export cars. The rear one also carried the stop and tail lamp and was left on the export cars, except late-model North American specification TCs. The front plate had a raised lip round the edge, and should correctly be hung so that the top is level with the front of the front apron. There were different types of rear backing plates. On the TA, there was an 'ear' for the round tail lamp at one end of the plate and the other end was square. On the TB and TC, the plate had both ends squared off. Some reproduction rear backing plates have two rounded-off ends which suits present-day installation of two D-shape lamps and looks quite neat.

INTERIOR TRIM AND HOOD

The seat had a one-piece squab but there were two seat cushions, individually adjustable on slides on the floorboards. The early TA model with body type B.269 had a rather tiresome squab adjustment where you had to re-position the squab manually, dowels on the bottom of the squab fitting into different holes in two racks on the floor; on body type B.270 and on the TC, the squab was hinged to the cushions. At the top, the squab was attached to the body with a quadrant on either side, adjustable by wing nuts. On the TA and TB, the quadrants were mounted on the inner sides of the rear wheel arches; on the TC, they were on top of the wheel arches.

TA and TB seats were constructed with horsehair padding over a spring base. On some cars, the cushions also incorporated Moseley 'Float-on-Air' inflatable rubber cushions, which you pumped up with a bicycle pump. They are likely to have perished on most cars. The TC had solid sponge rubber or Dunlopillo cushions. On later TCs, the rear of the cushions were recessed into the bottom of the squab; on earlier cars, the cushions simply butted up to the squab. The seat was upholstered in Connolly's 'Vaumol' leather on the TA and TB, and 'Celestra' leather on the TC. The back of the seat squab was covered in Rexine leathercloth, supposedly black on the pre-war cars but matching the upholstery colour on the TC. The later TCs also had Rexine on the inner sides and the back edges of the seat cushions, where the earlier cars had leather all round. The extra width of the TC was revealed in the seat squab, which had 22 flutes, apart from a narrower flute at each end. The TA and TB only had 20 flutes and the end flutes. The seat cushions always had eight flutes each. The seat back and the bottoms were of five-ply plywood.

release lever on top of the lock. Each door had two sidescreen mounting points, at the back in a socket within the thickness of the door, at the front on the door trims. The front mounting points were chrome-plated with a one-winged fastening nut. Their backing plates were round on pre-war cars, rectangular on the TC. At the bottom of each door opening was an aluminium sill plate, originally neatly lettered with the legend 'The M.G. Car Company Ltd.'. Later TCs had plain sill plates without lettering.

The floorcovering was black carpet, Courtauld's 'Karvel' with a rubberized hessian back. The edges were not originally bound, except the area immediately behind the gear lever. The propshaft tunnel was carpeted, but the gearbox tunnel was only carpeted on early TAs; other cars had a moulded rubber cover over the gearbox and remote control. On the driver's side was a rubber heel mat with an outward-facing MG octagon. The carpet was secured with lift-the-dot fasteners and press studs and was laid over a felt underlay which did not extend to the toeboard or propshaft tunnel. The heelboard (the vertical panel just behind the seat) was not carpeted but was painted black, and the starting handle was attached to the heelboard with clips. The bottom of the tonneau may have had a rubber mat on some pre-war cars, and was covered by carpet on the TC. At the rear of the tonneau was a vertical compartment for the sidescreens. This was lined with black felt and had a Rexine-covered flap hinged at the bottom, fastened with a strap at the top.

right
The style of door trim panels and door furniture changed very little from model to model in the T-series range. However, on pre-war cars such as this TA (blue trim), the front sidescreen mounting point had a small round backing plate like this. On the TC (red trim) there was a much bigger rectangular backing plate. The door locks were similar on all cars, and should not have the small locking lever seen here.

The door panels and side trim panels were in thin plywood. Originally the door panels were trimmed in leather, but some time during the TC's career Rexine was substituted. Rexine was used on the other trim panels on all cars. For the restorer who craves absolute originality, Rexine is likely to be a bit of a headache – there is no comparably awful quality vinyl on the market now! The door panels each had a map pocket following the shape of the door, and the top edge of the pocket was always in leather, even on Rexine-trimmed door panels. Around the edge of the door was a stitched beading, hiding the panel pins, and so commonly called a 'hidem banding'. Chrome-plated Wilmot Breeden Silent Travel door locks were fitted on the door trims, with a

left
Many reproduction hood covers have piping in a contrast colour, which is not authentic. The piping on the TA hood should be black rather than grey.

right
The TC usually had a fawn hood, although black may have been used on a few cars. Again, it must be pointed out that the colour of the piping should match the hood fabric. Note the characteristic line of the top of the sidescreens – virtually a straight line sloping down from front to rear. On the TC, the hood frame was painted light grey at first, later tan.

Under the dashboard was found a masking panel or baffleboard made from black millboard, stretching all the way forward to the toeboard and from side to side of the scuttle. The steering column had to be taken out to remove the panel; for this reason it has often been left out on restored cars, to give easier access to the wiring behind the dashboard. The áccelerator pedal, mounted on the toeboard, had a roller-type hard rubber or ebonite pad.

The hood and sidescreens were made from twill or single duck, black on pre-war cars, and usually fawn on the TC. Similarly, the hood and sidescreen frames were painted black on pre-war cars, and light grey or tan on the TC. There were two sidescreens on each side: the front sidescreen was mounted on the door and the rear sidescreen formed a quarterlight. The actual windows were from mica or celluloid, with a chrome-plated beading round their edges. This beading hid the bolts used to attach the sidescreens to their frames. A metal stiffener was sandwiched in the fabric material round the lower portion of the sidescreens. The lower half of the front sidescreens pivoted outwards, permitting the driver to signal his intentions. A strap secured the signalling flap to the inside door panel, with a lift-the-dot on pre-war cars and a press stud on TC and later cars.

The hood frame had two bows and was attached to the inside of the body, at the top just behind the seat squab. The hood cover had a narrow celluloid rear window, originally split in two with a central vertical dividing strip, but in 1948 the TC was given a larger, one-piece rear window. At the back, the hood cover was tacked to the rear top rail of the body. A press stud on each side secured the corner flaps. When the hood was erected, dowels on the top of the windscreen frame fitted into holes on the hood front rail which was then held in place by two chrome-plated wing nut fasteners on the inside of the hood. Neither the hood nor the tonneau cover had the contrast colour piping sometimes seen on modern reproductions.

The standard tonneau cover supplied with these cars was just that, only covering the area behind the seats. On pre-war cars it was made from black Rexine, also seen on early post-war cars. From approximately TC/5178 (in 1948), the tonneau cover was made from the same material as the hood. The tonneau cover was secured with four lift-the-dot fasteners below the edge of the hood. There was one on each side of the petrol tank, and one on each side of the body, in the top corner behind the door. The front of the tonneau cover was tucked over the black-painted tonneau rail on the back of the seat squab, and was held in place by elastic straps and lift-the-dots about halfway down the squab. The tonneau cover had small leather patches for reinforcement around holes for the rear sidescreen mounting points, to permit the use of sidescreens with the hood down and the tonneau cover in place. A full-length tonneau cover with a central zip was optional before the war but does not seem to have been offered on the TC when new.

right
The hood cover was permanently attached to the rear top rail of the body and was fastened with a press stud in the corner by the rear sidescreen. The divided, narrow rear window was found on all cars until modified on the TC in 1948.

below
This detail shot shows the correct shape and size of the rear window.

bottom
Pre-war cars and early TCs had black tonneau covers, but a fawn tonneau cover was introduced in 1948. It was held in place by four lift-the-dot fasteners like the one seen here. The semi-circular leather patch reinforces the area round the hole for the rear sidescreen mounting point. This patch, and the piping, should correctly also be fawn.

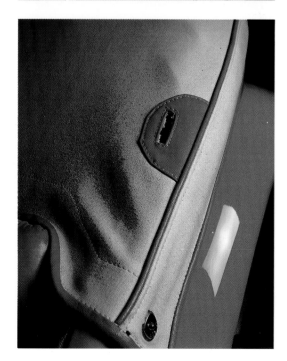

DASHBOARD AND INSTRUMENTS

The layout of the dashboard was broadly similar on all models including the Tickford coupé. The facia panel was plywood covered in walnut veneer. Two types of veneer were found: either in one piece with horizontal grain, or in two pieces with a symmetrical grain pattern. In 1948 the TC acquired a Rexine-covered dashboard, from approximately TC/5380. This was coloured to match the upholstery and trim. On the Rexine-covered dashboard, cup washers were added to the screws holding the dashboard in place. Around the panel was chrome-plated beading, with Rexine piping between the dashboard and the scuttle. This piping continued downwards on either side along the door shutline, between the door pillar and the trim panel on the side of the scuttle.

The instruments were grouped symmetrically. Starting from the left, in front of the passenger was a 5in Jaeger chronometric speedometer, marked up to 100mph, with a five-figure total distance recorder (top) and a three-figure plus decimal trip recorder (below), with a re-setting button below the dashboard. Kilometres speedometers were fitted to export cars, as required. Next to the speedometer was a Lucas DF41 map reading lamp, with a chrome-plated housing and a black painted base. It was switched on by turning the lamp housing.

In the centre of the dashboard was a Lucas instrument panel, made from chrome-plated sheet brass but painted black so the chrome-plating showed only on the edge. In this panel were set a Lucas ammeter (reading to +/− 20 amp), followed by a Lucas combined ignition and lighting switch. On the TA and TB this switch also had two positions for high and low charge, not necessary on the TC with its automatic voltage regulator. The ignition lock had a Wilmot Breeden barrel with a key number in the MRN range. Next came a Lucas combined horn push and dip switch, and finally a Jaeger oil pressure gauge. Below was a row of minor controls, with the function of each being marked in horizontal lettering on the panel directly above it. Again going from left to right, they were the starter pull, the mixture (choke) control, the fog lamp switch, a two-pin plug socket for an inspection lamp, the panel light switch, and a screw-type slow running control or hand throttle. All switches and knobs were black.

To the right of the central panel was a Lucas 'Thirtilite' device which matched the map reading lamp. This lit up green when the speed was between 20 and 30mph and went out again when one exceeded 30mph. Export cars had an additional map reading lamp in this position. In 1948, the colour of the instrument panel and of the bases of the map reading lamp and 'Thirtilite' was changed from black to a metallic tan or bronze colour, probably at the time when the Rexine-covered dashboard was introduced.

In front of the driver was a 5in Jaeger rev

The dashboard was very similar on all models. This TA has the correct horizontal lettering above the switches on the instrument panel. The grab handle is likely to be a contemporary accessory. The Brooklands steering wheel was not a factory fitment either, and the mottled brown rim on this wheel would be more correct on a post-war car. The water temperature gauge on the extreme right was a factory-fitted option.

above
This TB is fitted with a black-rimmed Brooklands wheel which is more correct on a pre-war car. This car has the early type of gear lever knob, with the engraved 'gate' surrounding the gear positions. This mushroom-shaped knob was replaced by a pear-shaped knob seen on all post-war T-types.

At first glance the TC dashboard is identical to that of the pre-war cars, but closer inspection reveals that the petrol tap has been replaced by a low petrol level warning lamp, to the right of the rev counter. The tax disc holder with the MG badge, a type often supplied by the factory on home market cars, is a particularly nice touch.

counter (tachometer) which was driven off a reduction box on the dynamo. It read to 6500rpm with no red line indicated. At the bottom of the rev counter dial was a clock. On the TA and TB this was a mechanical eight-day clock, and the dial was integral with the main dial of the rev counter. The TC was fitted with an electric clock, with a separate clock dial. In both cases the resetting (or winding) button protruded below the edge of the dashboard. Finally, to the right of the steering column was the petrol tap with two positions, main and reserve (no off position). This was black with white lettering. On the TC it was replaced by a green warning lamp marked 'Fuel' which started to flash when there were around three gallons left in the tank.

All the instruments were set in chrome-plated rims, and had silver-grey dials with dark brown figures and pointers. There was some variation in the colour of the dials, and it would seem that over the years the colour gradually became a darker silver-grey with a greener hue. The instruments had rim lighting, through apertures in the rim between the dials and the glasses. Green translucent celluloid in the lighting apertures gave that ghostly green glow mentioned in contemporary accounts!

opposite
A worthwhile alternative to the open two-seater, the Tickford drophead coupé was an equally attractive motor car, and somewhat better finished.

left
The instruments were little changed but it is possible to distinguish this as a pre-war rev counter because the clock dial is integral with the main dial. This is in fact a TB.

below
This speedometer is also from the TB. These instruments are typical of the colour found on many T Series instruments, but some slight variation did occur.

The central instrument panel was originally painted black but was changed to metallic tan or bronze in 1948. This TC is likely to have been fitted with a reproduction panel, as the lettering above the controls is missing. The bezel for the light switch seen here is an incorrect type. It should be plain black, without a window, and should have white lettering 'OFF-S-H'. Pre-war cars also had an adjustment for high and low charge on the light switch.

opposite
Dark blue was not a standard colour on the Tickford, and typically the hood colour would match the paint colour on a TA Tickford such as this. Fawn hoods only came in with the TB model.

TICKFORD DROPHEAD COUPÉ BODY (TA & TB)

The Tickford coupé body was supplied by Salmons and Sons Ltd of Newport Pagnell in Buckinghamshire, a company that is still happily in existence as an off-shoot of Aston Martin Lagonda. Their records list 240 home market deliveries of TA and TB coupés, but with export deliveries and 'missing' chassis numbers it is likely that there were as many as 320 cars (260 TAs and 60 TBs). The first Tickford bodied car was TA/2184, which started life in chassis form in March 1938 and was completed by Salmons in June, although the new model was not revealed publicly before August 1938. Production continued until August 1939. Although early post-war Tickford advertising 'flew a kite' by showing drawings of what a Tickford TC might look like – with skirted front wings – no such car was ever built.

Apart from the MG chassis and engine numbers, the Tickfords were identified by a Salmons 'job number'. This was stamped on the back of the interior wooden trim pieces, on the back of the hood irons, and on an aluminium strip on the toolbox lid. As these numbers vary from at least 3673 to 5316, they must have been taken from a series shared by all Salmons-built bodies and are therefore not a guide to the production figures of the MG Midget coupés. (Salmons also made Tickford drophead bodies for the SA, VA and WA MG models of the 1936–39 period.)

The Midget drophead coupé was rather more civilised than the two-seater, and as one might expect carried a weight penalty of 2cwt (approximately 100kg): the TB two-seater weighed in at 15½cwt, the coupé at 17½cwt. Starting at the front end, the Tickford normally had the radiator slats painted body (as opposed to upholstery) colour, and there was a moulding along the sides of the bonnet top panels to match up with a moulding on the scuttle side and along the top of the door. The Tickford was the one TA or TB model that did have trafficators as standard, built into the sides of the scuttle. The aperture may or may not have a beading round it. The Lucas trafficators had chrome-plated arms.

The windscreen pillars were fixed and painted body colour, but the chrome-plated windscreen frame (made by Perfecta of Birmingham) was hinged at the top and opened up to a horizontal position. It was adjusted on two quadrants with knurled finger nuts. The doors were full height and incorporated wind-down windows, the winders being chrome-plated with ebonite knobs in either of two different styles. The driver's door had an external key-operated lock, with the locking barrel set in the MG octagon of the door handle. While the handles were similar to those found on two-seaters, the octagonal escutcheons were different, not being elongated. However, some cars had the elongated octagonal escutcheon.

The doors were wider than the two-seater doors, and had a cut-out to allow for the curve of

above
Opinions differ on the Ace wheel discs found on this particular car. However, if they are fitted, one would normally expect the spare wheel to be fitted with a disc as well.

The external mirror from the two-seater was replaced on later Tickfords by an internal one. This was the only T-type to be fitted with trafficators as standard. In this and the previous photograph, the moulding along the bonnet, the scuttle and the door can be seen clearly. The door handles on this car are not the correct type -- they should be the same as on the two-seater, but with an external key-operated lock on the driver's side.

above
Instead of the fold-flat windscreen of the two-seater, the Tickford had a fixed windscreen frame. The top-hinged windscreen could be opened right up to this horizontal position. Note the wipers mounted on the scuttle.

The door trims incorporated map pockets, although most cars had plain pockets with an elasticated top, rather than the fluting seen here. The strip below the pocket is the coachbuilder's name plate.

the rear wing at the bottom rear edge. They were supported on three body-colour hinges each. The door windows were guided in chrome-plated channels front and rear; the rear one was hinged and could be folded down within the thickness of the door when the window was wound fully down. The inside door trim panels were finished at the top with a walnut garnish rail which matched the dashboard rail at the rear edge of the scuttle. The internal door locks were similar to those found on the two-seater, but sat upon alloy backing plates ⅛in thick which compensated for the thickness of the trim panels. In each door trim panel was a slight recess with a map pocket, which had an elasticated top.

Interior trim was generally to a higher standard than on the two-seater. There were two individually adjustable bucket-type seats with forward hinging squabs. The seats incorporated 'Float-on-Air' cushions. Seat upholstery and door trims were leather with a range of colours different from the two-seater. The back of the seat squabs and the edges of the frame of the seat bases were carpeted. Wilton carpeting (with bound edges) in colours to tone with the upholstery was used. On some cars the gearbox tunnel was carpeted, and so were the inner sides of the scuttle. An extra map pocket may be found on the passenger's side of the scuttle. The rear wheel arches, the heelboard, and the back panel of the tonneau were fully carpeted. The bottom of the luggage area in the tonneau was covered by a rubber mat.

The top of the scuttle was flat on the coupé and finished with a walnut garnish rail. The dashboard was recessed under the scuttle and was a different shape to that on the two-seater, although the layout was broadly similar. The dashboard was made from solid walnut (except on the car photographed for this book!) and had chrome-plated end pieces. The speedometer and rev counter were moved down and outwards, and the petrol tap was re-located on a bracket behind the dashboard. One additional control on the coupé was the trafficator switch, either with a warning lamp or of the self-cancelling type, which took the place of the map reading lamp on the two-seater.

On the coupé, the wiper motor was mounted on the left-hand side of the bulkhead under the bonnet, outboard of the toolbox, and the wipers were mounted below the windscreen. The wipers were individually controlled from two knobs on the dashboard rail. In the centre of this was an ash tray. Early Tickfords had an external mirror

similar to the two-seater mirror, but later cars were fitted with a small internal mirror mounted centrally below the windscreen.

The outer hood cover was mohair, available in a variety of colours. The hood was fully lined, and between outer cover and lining was a layer of rubberized waterproof material. The hood was of the three-position type, where the front part could be rolled back and secured with straps in the 'de-ville' position. For this purpose the cant rails above the side windows were folded back under the hood. These cant rails and the vertical hood pillars behind the side windows were painted body colour. Once the front portion had been folded, the hood irons were broken and the entire hood folded back. Even in the folded position the hood sat some way above the line of the body.

At the bottom of the hood, where it was attached to the rear of the body, was chrome-plated brass pin beading. There was also chrome-plated brass beading around the letterbox-slit glass

above left
The interior was more luxurious, with two individual seats. Note the correct finish, with carpeting to the edge of the seat bottom.

above
The backs of the seats were covered in carpet, and so were the panels lining the tonneau. The actual luggage platform would most likely have been covered by a rubber mat. Note that the starting handle is clipped to the carpet-covered heelboard. The straps hanging from the hood are for fastening the front part of the hood and the cant rails when folded back. The interior lamp shown here is not quite the correct type.

The layout of the dashboard is little different from the two-seater. Most Tickfords had a solid walnut dashboard, but this unique painted dashboard is believed to be original to this particular car. The trafficator switch takes the place of the map reading light. As the scuttle is flat, the major instruments are moved downwards and outwards, and the petrol tap has therefore been displaced to a bracket behind the dashboard. The wiper controls and the ash tray can be seen on the dashboard rail.

rear window, which measured approximately 3½in by 20in. An external mirror was a good idea whether the hood was up or down! An interior lamp was fitted above the rear window on the transverse hoodstick.

At least 133 original Tickfords survive. This is a considerable proportion of the total number made but is naturally insignificant compared to the number of surviving two-seaters. Patterns for the carpets, upholstery, interior trim panels and hood all exist or have been re-created, and many items of body trim had been reproduced, often by owners who have restored their cars. Complete body tubs have also been made: Naylor Brothers made a batch of 10 some years ago, and the Cooke Group (of Wigston in Leicestershire) has made two.

left
Salmons' patent number plate is attached to the top of the windscreen frame.

below left
The hood fabric is attached at the back with this chrome-plate covered pin beading. There should probably also have been a chrome-plated finisher across the hood, on the hood bow above the rear window.

below
The 'pram irons' are more correctly called landau irons.

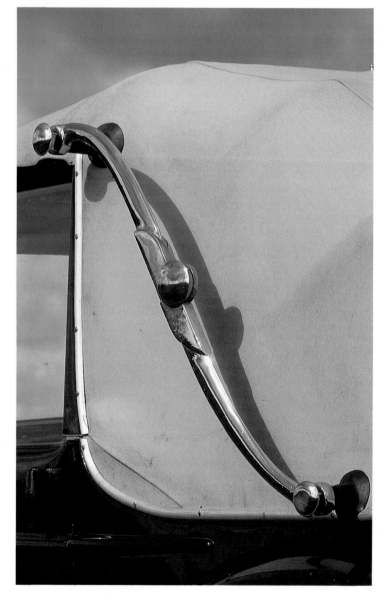

This is the first stage of folding the hood back: the front portion is rolled up, and tied up together with the folded-back cant rails . . .

below
. . . as can be seen in this photograph of the completely folded hood. Note how the landau irons have been broken open and folded back, and that the rear window channel has been folded forward into the door above the wound-down window.

EXPORT VARIATIONS

Before the war, export variations were limited such minor details as the provision of a kilometr speedometer, double-dipping headlamps and th change-over in the positions of the horn, fog an tail lamps, all detailed in previous sections. A fev TAs were sent to Australia in chassis-only forn and were built up with locally made bodies although these were probably similar to the standard two-seater bodies. Similarly a few TAs were sent to Eire in 'unassembled' form – what we would now call CKD (Completely Knocked Down) exports – and after the war 84 TCs exported in CKD form were assembled by Messrs Booth Bros Ltd in Dublin (who later also assembled TDs and TFs). It is unlikely that these cars differed greatly from the standard Abingdon assembled cars.

With the TC, a series of distinctly different export versions were recognised. The basic right-hand drive export TC (type 'EXR') had double-dipping headlamps with twin-filament bulbs to both lamps, an extra map reading lamp in place of the 'Thirtilite' and a rear view mirror positioned centrally above the dashboard. With the addition of a kilometres speedometer this model became type 'EXR/K'. However, these codes were not added to the chassis number on the guarantee plate, but all export cars did have an extra plate with the MG badge and the words 'Made in England'.

In 1948, a special model was evolved for sale to the USA (and, presumably, Canada; some such cars were delivered in Britain for Personal Export, or may have gone to other markets). Early TCs exported to North America were more or less to standard export specification. Some were fitted with bumper guards, which it is thought were added by American importers – either vertical rods front and rear, or simple horizontal full-width bumpers without overriders. However, contemporary pictures of TCs in Australia or South America also occasionally show these cars fitted with bumpers. In the USA, a few TCs were re-painted in two-tone colour schemes when new.

Feedback from the important American market led to Abingdon incorporating the following alterations in export cars for the USA which were then recognised under the coding 'EX-U' stamped with the chassis number on the guarantee plate:

- Full-width bumpers front and rear with overriders, and a central MG medallion to the rear bumper.

- Badge bar, fog lamp and external horn deleted.

- Two Lucas windtone horns, WT614 and WT615, mounted under the bonnet.

- Steering wheel in gold pearl finish instead of black.

- No 'Thirtilite', but two map reading lamps.

- Rear view mirror centrally mounted above the dashboard.

- Flashing direction indicator switch (Lucas SD84 with built-in warning lamp) in place of inspection lamp socket on dashboard.

- High beam warning lamp in place of fog lamp switch.

- Instrument panel re-arranged: ammeter and oil gauge mounted centrally, ignition and lighting switch on the outside left, horn push and dip switch on the outside right.

The fully-fledged 'EX-U' model came into being only in December 1948, from chassis number TC/7380, and only 494 such cars were made before the end of TC production. Nevertheless, statistics kept by Abingdon's Production Control Department claim that 2001 'North American' TCs were made from 1947 to 1949. We cannot be certain exactly how 1947 and 1948 cars to 'North American' specification differed from other TCs. These statistics have led to the oft-repeated assertion that 2001 was the number of TCs actually exported to the USA, but this can be proved to be incorrect. Both production and export statistics will be found later in this book.

IDENTIFICATION AND DATING (TA, TB AND TC)

The three models had chassis numbers prefixed with TA, TB and TC respectively, and the chassis number series began with 0251 for each model – as is probably well known, 251 was the telephone number of the MG factory. TA chassis numbers ran from TA/0251 to TA/3253; TB from TB/0251 to TB/0629; and TC from TC/0251 to TC/10251. The chassis number plate, or maker's guarantee plate, was found on the left-hand side of the front of the bulkhead-mounted toolbox on the TA and TB, while on the TC it was on the left-hand end of the battery box in front of the toolbox. The chassis number was also stamped on the frame itself, on the side of the chassis behind the left-hand dumb-iron. The only variation in the chassis number system was that TC cars to North American specification of 1948-49 had an additional code, 'EX-U', stamped with the chassis number on the maker's plate.

This plate was also stamped with the engine number. The two types of engine found each had their different prefix for the engine number – MPJG on the TA, XPAG on the TB and TC. In addition the engine number was found on a plate on the engine itself. The TA had a round plate on the right-hand side of the crankcase, the TB and TC an octagonal plate on the top of the bell housing, visible from the left-hand side. TA engine numbers started from 501 and ran up to at least 3503. TB engine numbers also started from 501 and ran up to 883, with TC engine numbers following in the same sequence, from 884 to at least 10923.

Finally each car had a body number. The body number plate was attached to the left-hand (passenger side) body pillar inside the scuttle. This plate carried a body type number, which was B.269 (1936-37 TAs with narrow rear wings), B.270 (1937-39 TAs with wide rear wings, and TBs), B.278 (TA and TB Tickford coupés), or B.280 (TCs). No records exist of the body numbers for individual cars, but it is thought that the B.269 body numbers for the early TAs ran from 100 to 1090, with the B.270 body numbers also starting with 100. The body number stamped on the plate was followed by the body maker's batch number. Please refer to the Tickford section for a description of the Salmons Tickford body job numbers.

As previously mentioned, TC export cars carried a special 'Made in England' plate adjacent to the chassis number plate. All TCs also had a patent number plate, listing the numbers of patents embodied in the construction of the car.

The following list of first chassis numbers issued in each year is taken from the ledgers giving the dates of issue of guarantee plates to each car (found in the archives of the MG Car Club). Although these dates are slightly earlier than the actual production dates, they are nevertheless a good guide to dating individual cars.

As far as the TC is concerned, the annual production figures implied by this series of chassis numbers do not quite match the figures compiled by Abingdon's Production Control Department found in the next section of this book. The reason is that the guarantee plates were usually issued at the start of the production process and this is reflected in the dates in the guarantee plate ledgers, but Production Control only counted a car towards their statistics when it came off the line, which could be several days later. Owners of TCs in Britain who wish to claim the concessionary rate of annual vehicle excise duty for their vehicles, applicable if the cars were manufactured before 1 January 1947, should note that TC/2051 is definitely the highest chassis number which can in any way be documented as having been issued in 1946!

It is worth pointing out (and this applies to all T-types) that the engine and body numbers were not issued in strict numerical order by the sequence of chassis numbers, therefore the difference between the chassis number and the engine number will vary between cars of the same model. As far as the pre-war cars were concerned, if a car was fitted with a replacement engine by the factory when new or nearly new, quite often a new guarantee plate with the new engine number would be issued. Several examples of TA cars with such engine changes can be documented in the guarantee plate ledger. These replacement engines appear also to have had the MPJG prefix. Reconditioned factory replacement engines fitted in post-war years tend to have five-figure numbers, prefixed with A if of standard bore size, B if first overbore size, etc.

TA	June 1936	TA/0253	(first production TA; 0251 and 0252 were prototypes)
	January 1937	TA/1016	
	January 1938	TA/2044	
	March 1938	TA/2187	(first chassis for Tickford coupé)
	January 1939	TA/3061	
	April 1939	TA/3253	(the last TA)
TB	May 1939	TB/0253	(first production TB; 0251 and 0252 were prototypes)
	October 1939	TB/0629	(the last TB)
TC	September 1945	TC/0252	(first production TC; 0251 was a prototype)
	January 1946	TC/0352	
	January 1947	TC/2052	
	January 1948	TC/4412	
	January 1949	TC/7503	
	November 1949	TC/10251	(the last TC)

PRODUCTION CHANGES (TA, TB & TC)

The number in the first column is either a chassis number (prefix TA, TB or TC) or an engine number (prefix MPJG for the TA, XPAG for the TB and TC).

MPJG/684   (Aug 1936)
Synchromesh in place of 'crash' gearbox

MPJG/697   (Aug 1936)
Three-ring pistons in place of four-ring pistons.

TA/0652   (Sep 1936)
Modified engine fume pipe.

MPJG/1048   (Oct 1936)
Oil cup on water pump in place of Stauffer greaser.

TA/0824   (Nov 1936)
Modified petrol tap and pipe from tap to pump.

MPJG/1139   (Nov 1936)
Modified oil filter cover.

MPJG/1294   (Jan 1937)
Modified clutch cover plate.

TA/1250 (approx)   (Apr 1937)
Body type B.270 replaced body type B.269 (for details, see bodywork section).

MPJG/1514   (May 1937)
New type of oil filter; separate oil delivery pipe from filter to block deleted.

TA/1306   (May 1937)
Return spring fitted to hand-brake cross shaft.

MPJG/1605   (May 1937)
Triple instead of double valve springs.

TA/1770   (Oct 1937)
Side-laced in place of centre-laced wire wheels.

TA/1877   (Oct 1937)
Modified carburettor controls.

TA/1926   (Nov 1937)
Modified carburettor suction chambers.

TA/1990   (Dec 1937)
Return spring fitted to slow running control.

TA/2187   (Mar 1938)
First chassis to be fitted with Tickford body.

TA/2232   (Mar 1938)
Flexible section added to oil pressure gauge feed line.

TA/2253   (Mar 1938)
Grouped chassis lubrication nipples introduced. Individual greasers on spring trunnions and brake cables ceased with TA/2252.

TA/2254   (Mar 1938)
New type of front spring with seven leaves.

MPJG/2514   (Mar 1938)
Rubber spacer for plug leads deleted.

MPJG/2592   (Apr 1938)
Water pump spindle located with peg.

MPJG/2622   (Apr 1938)
Oil deflecting plate added to front of camshaft.

TA/2486   (Jun 1938)
Clutch pedal bracket fitted with clevis pin.

TA/2518   (Jul 1938)
All chassis grease nipples changed from Enot to Tecalemit. New type of grease gun in tool kit.

MPJG/2847   (Aug 1938)
Modified valve spring cap with packing ring.

MPJG/3053   (Oct 1938)
Modified rocker shaft bracket supports.

TA/2882   (Nov 1938)
Telescopic steering wheel fitted to two-seater (always found on drophead coupé). Steering box ratio altered from 8:1 to 11:1.

TA/3208   (Mar 1939)
Coupé only: internal mirror in place of external one.

There were a number of modifications on the TA which appear in the Service Parts List but which cannot be directly related to a chassis or engine number, as the change point given relates to the number of the component or sub-assembly:

From front axle no. 1501:
New type of king pin with felt washer.

From front axle no. 2154:
Introduction of bolt anchor bracket for steering knuckle and steering arm.

From rear axle no. 1501:
Modified bevel pinion housing and bearings.

From rear axle no. 2501:
Propshaft flange nuts increased from ½in BSF to ⅝in BSF.

From body no. 507 (B.269):
Carpet over gearbox replaced by moulded rubber cover (possibly around TA/0658, Sep 1936).

From body no.1790 (B.270):
D-shaped tail lamp and new rear number plate (possibly around TA/3200, Mar 1939, *or* from the start of the TB).

The modifications made to the TB over the TA have been described in detail in the appropriate sections of the text. There were not very many modifications made to the TB during its short production run, but the Service Parts List indicates the following:

TB/0307   (May 1939)
Modified crankshaft pulley.

XPAG/645   (June 1939)
Revised design of tappet cover and studs for same.

Again, the modifications made to the TC from the outset of production in 1945 are listed in the text. During the TC's production run the following modifications were made to the TC, in so far as they can be referred to a chassis or engine number:

XPAG/2020   (Sep 1946)
Cast aluminium rocker cover, incorporating oil filler with clamp, replaced pressed steel rocker cover with snap-on oil filler.

TC/1850   (Nov 1946)
Diamond pattern headlamp introduced as replacement for, or alternative to, horseshoe pattern.

TC/2196   (Jan 1947)
Speedometer cable re-routed, cable housing improved.

XPAG/2966   (Feb 1947)
Cast aluminium rocker cover discontinued, original pressed steel rocker cover re-introduced.

TC/3414   (Aug 1947)
Control box changed from Lucas RF91 to RF95/2.

TC/3856   (Oct 1947)
Hydraulic piston dampers added to carburettors.

TC/4251   (Dec 1947)
Tapered packing pieces added between front axle and springs, reducing castor angle from 8° to 5½°.

TC/4739   (Feb 1948)
Fog lamp changed from Lucas FT27 to SFT462. Revised design of tail lamp.

TC/5000 (approx)   (Mar 1948)
Body-coloured bulkhead and red engine introduced.

TC/5039   (Mar 1948)
Redesigned steering box drop arm.

TC/5086 (approx)   (Mar 1948)
Plain instead of lettered sill tread plates.

TC/5178 (approx)   (Apr 1948)
Fawn instead of black tonneau cover.

TC/5380 (approx)   (Apr 1948)
Rexine-covered dashboard replaced walnut veneer dashboard. Instrument panel in metallic tan with black lettering replaced black panel with white lettering.

TC/7380   (Dec 1948)
Introduction of 'EX-U' model with modifications as detailed in the section on export variations.

There were a number of modifications to the TC which cannot be referred to a specific change point by chassis or engine number. As previously described in the section on the interior trim, there were two different types of seat and the door trim panels changed from leather to Rexine, in 1946 or 1948 depending on who you believe! There is also some argument among the experts over the front wings. Early TC wings had a deeper cut-back to the swan-neck at the leading edge of the wing where it swept down to meet the dumb-iron; this wing was shaped like that of the pre-war cars. On later models, the cut-back was reduced, pulling the edge of the wing further forward. There was also a change to the hood frame side members, which had an off-set at the front on early cars, missing on later cars.

OPTIONAL EXTRAS (TA & TB)

The following 'approved extras' were offered on the TA and TB:

Aero screen, one or two (two-seater only).
Bonnet strap.
Bulb carrier.
Battery acid level indicators.
Cigar lighter.
Double-dipping headlamps (for Continental use).
Fire extinguisher (Pyrene Junior).
Full-length tonneau cover with zip (two-seater only).
Inspection lamp.
Luggage carrier (two-seater only).
Master battery switch.
Number plates in aluminium (pair).
Oil thermometer.
Radiator shield, in black or colour.
Radio, 'Philco', six or seven valve types.
Radio aerial, telescopic type.
Reversing lamp.
Second spare wheel (less tyre and tube).
Second spare wheel attachment.
Trafficators (two-seater only; standard on coupé).
Water thermometer.

The oil and water thermometer matched the size of the oil pressure gauge and ammeter, and were of similar design and colouring to the other instruments. If fitted they were set at the two extremities of the dashboard.

For details of special colour and trim finishes, please see the section on colour schemes.

OPTIONAL EXTRAS (TC)

It seems that the list of options was drastically pruned after the war; if you wanted a TC, you had to take it or leave it as it came! I have only been able to verify the following extras being quoted:

Luggage carrier.
'Radiomobile' radio (installed under the dashboard).

The absence of a full-length tonneau cover was remarked upon in a road test of the TC in *The Motor* in 1947, and was ascribed to the then-current shortage of material.

COMPETITION PARTS (TA)

The following competition parts were listed for this model:

High compression ratio cylinder head (7.3:1).
Stiffer valve springs.
Bracket to raise oil filter 2½in, with pipes.
Steel sump
Two alternative sets of lower gearbox ratios.
Special front springs.
Lower rear axle ratio of 5.375:1 (8/43).
Brake tandem master cylinder.
Special hand throttle (slow running) control.
Twin independent petrol pumps, with control switch.
Larger shock absorbers, or Luvax P.6 piston type shock absorbers.
Square rear number plate and competition number board.
Spare sparking plug carrier.
4.00-16 wheels with 6.00-16 tyres, or 4.50-16 wheels with 6.50- 16 tyres.
Cycle type wings and special side fairings, in steel or aluminium.
Aluminium bonnet with louvres to bonnet tops.
Supercharger assembly and special carburettor.

Most of these parts were undoubtedly aimed at the trials fraternity wishing to emulate the successes achieved by the factory-sponsored TA trials teams, notably the 'Cream Crackers' and the 'Three Musketeers'. Actually these two teams' cars mostly used 1548cc MG VA engines, or even the over-bored 1700cc version of the VA engine.

COMPETITION PARTS (TB & TC)

For a detailed description of tuning of the XPAG engine, please see the section which appears later in this book. Many of the non-engine parts listed above for the TA were undoubtedly also available for the TB, but were probably not available after the war. It is, however, worth mentioning that the TB and TC could be equipped with a higher final drive ratio of 4.875:1 (8/39) as found on the TA, and the wider 16in wheel continued to be available for the TB and TC models.

PRODUCTION AND EXPORT FIGURES (TA & TB)

No particularly detailed production figures exist for the pre-war MG cars, so the following table for TA and TB models has been based solely on the guarantee plate issue ledgers. The split between two-seaters and coupés has been based on the figure of 320 Tickford-bodied cars. The dates assigned to Tickford cars are the dates of issue of the guarantee plates, not the dates when these cars were completed by Salmons. Officially there were no chassis-only deliveries, other than for export, mainly to Australia. Such cars have been counted as two-seaters, as have the unassembled cars exported to Eire. The resulting figures are as follows:

	1936	1937	1938	1939	Total, all years	
TA two-seater	763	1028	794	156	2741	
TA Airline coupé	2	—	—	—	2	} 3003
TA drophead coupé	—	—	223	37	260	
TB two-seater	—	—	—	319	319	} 379
TB drophead coupé	—	—	—	60	60	
All models	**765**	**1028**	**1017**	**572**	**3382**	

At this time MG's export sales were handled by Nuffield Exports Limited, and calendar year statistics exist from 1937 onwards. According to this, the major export markets were as follows (no split possible between TA and TB):

	1937	1938	1939	1940	Total, all years	
Australia	49	24	34	6	113	(incl. 10 chassis)
Germany	25	30	24	0	79	(incl. 13 d/h coupés)
Malaya	20	11	9	7	47	
S. Africa and Rhodesia	10	9	8	3	30	
Belgium	12	3	1	0	16	
Switzerland	8	5	3	0	16	
Eire	8	4	0	0	12	
Netherlands	4	3	4	1	12	
Canada	11	0	0	0	11	
Hong Kong	3	2	0	6	11	
USA	6	3	1	1	11	
Denmark	2	5	3	0	10	
New Zealand	6	2	1	0	9	
Sweden	8	1	0	0	9	
Argentina	2	3	1	2	8	
Total of above	**174**	**105**	**89**	**26**	**394**	
Total of all exports	**212**	**126**	**107**	**27**	**472**	
(of which d/h coupés)		(3)	(28)		(31)	

It seems likely that around 100 further cars were exported during 1936.

PRODUCTION AND EXPORT FIGURES (TC)

The single TC prototype (which was probably a re-worked TB, the 1939–40 works demonstrator registered CJB 59) had chassis number 0251. Production cars commenced with 0252 and ran to 10251, which equals 10000 cars made. The following statistics were kept by the Production Control Department in the Abingdon factory.

	1945	1946	1947	1948	1949	Total, all years
Home market	34	1001	1146	297	930	3408
Export, RHD	47	638	1194★	1278	1340	4497
Export, North America	0	0	6	1473	522	2001
Chassis only, RHD	0	0	0	1	9	10
CKD cars, RHD	0	36	0	36	12	84 (for Eire)
All specifications	**81**	**1675**	**2346**	**3085**	**2813**	**10000**

CKD cars – Completely Knocked Down kit cars which were assembled abroad.

★In 1947, Abingdon quoted 1026 RHD export cars and 168 *LHD* export cars. As the TC was never made with left-hand drive this must be a mistake! In the table above, these 168 cars have been counted together with the RHD export cars; however, they may have been to a special specification, for example for the USA.

The following were the major export markets, according to Nuffield Exports statistics:

	1945	1946	1947	1948	1949	Total, all years
USA	0	20	234	1143	423	1820
Australia	2	108	165	599	900	1774
S. Africa and Rhodesia	0	83	139	241	154	617
Switzerland	2	59	142	130	75	408
Canada	0	6	20	247	97	370
Belgium	0	27	122	104	33	286
Malaya	0	27	31	66	55	179
India and Pakistan	0	49	54	31	6	140
Argentina	10	70	24	1	0	105
Eire	6	0	36★	36★	12★	90 ★CKD
Brazil	0	0	3	55	6	64
West Germany	0	0	0	5	59	64
Sweden	0	10	50	0	0	60
Ceylon	0	19	11	8	8	46
Hong Kong	0	3	17	10	16	46
Egypt	0	19	10	10	5	44
Total of above	**20**	**500**	**1058**	**2686**	**1849**	**6113**
Total of all exports	**23**	**610**	**1162**	**2815**	**1983**	**6593**

COLOUR SCHEMES (TA & TB)

From 1936 to 1938, the following were the standard colours on the two-seater:

Saxe Blue, with Blue trim
Racing Green, with Green trim
Emgee Red (or possibly Carmine Red), with Red trim
Cream, with Red trim
Black, with Blue, Green, Biscuit or Red trim

The hood, sidescreens and tonneau cover were black. The carpets were black. The wheels were finished in silver.

In August 1938 the drophead coupé was launched and things became a great deal more complicated. The following were the standard colour schemes in 1938-39:

Paint	Trim, 2-str.	Hood, 2-str.	Trim, coupé	Hood, coupé
Saxe Blue	Blue	Black	Grey	Blue
Coral Red	Red	Black	Maroon	Red
Apple Green	Green	Black	Biscuit	Green
Duo-green	Biscuit	Black	Biscuit	Green
Maroon	Maroon	Black	Brown	Maroon
Light Grey	Grey	Black	Grey	Grey
Black	(any)	Black	(any)	Black
Metallic Grey	Grey	Black	Grey	Grey

Notes: Duo-green: Light green body, dark green wings and fairings.
Metallic Grey: Metallic on body, non-metallic on wings and fairings.

Carpets remained black on the two-seater but were to tone with the trim on the drophead coupé. Wheels were silver as standard but could be finished in special colours to order (cost £1.1.0 for the set). The drophead coupés could be fitted with hoods in special colours to choice from the standard range. It was possible to have a car finished in a two-tone scheme, in any combination of two standard colours, on the body and on the wings and fairings respectively. Cars could also be finished in any Nobel stock colour, including metallic finishes and white on the two-seaters, at extra cost. Trim could be chosen from any standard colour if desired, or in any colour from Connolly's 'Vaumol' range at extra cost.

The TB colour schemes were basically as for the late TAs. However, green trim was discontinued, replaced by biscuit trim on green two-seaters, and so was brown trim, replaced by maroon trim on maroon drophead coupés. Red and green hoods were replaced on TB drophead coupés in these colours by fawn hoods, and fawn was offered as an alternative hood colour on drophead coupés in all other body colours as well.

COLOUR SCHEMES (TC)

The colour range was much simplified after the war, to the extent that at first the TC was available only in black, with a choice of red, green or beige trim. In approximately September 1946, the following colours were added:

Red, with Red or Beige trim
Green, with Beige or Green trim

In 1947 or 1948, two more colours were added. The complete range was now:

Black, with Regency Red, Vellum Beige or Shires Green trim
MG Red, with Regency Red or Vellum Beige trim
Shires Green, with Vellum Beige or Shires Green trim
Sequoia Cream, with Regency Red or Shires Green trim
Clipper Blue, with Vellum Beige trim

There is, by the way, no suggestion that the paint or trim colours were changed; MG only adopted more fancy names for them.

The carpets were black, and the hood and sidescreens fawn (black on some cars). The tonneau cover was black, changed to fawn in 1948. The wheels were silver.

During 1949 the colour range was revised, and the following colours were used on the last TCs as well as on the TDs through to 1951 (see colour list later in this book):

Black, with Red, Beige or Green trim
MG Red, with Red or Beige trim
Almond Green, with Beige trim
Ivory, with Red or Green trim
Clipper Blue, with Beige trim

As has been pointed out previously (in the section on the TA/TB/TC cooling system), the radiator slats were painted to match the upholstery colour, but with some variation depending on whether the upholstery and trim were to tone with the body, or in a contrast colour.

The pre-war paints were supplied by the Nobel company (the dynamite people!) and it is likely that they would now be rather difficult to re-mix. I have never come across any mixing formulae, and the colours are not recognised by present-day paint manufacturers. Attempts have been made at correlating these old colours to BMC colours of the 1950s and 1960s, but I believe this can only result in approximations. The best solution might be to try to match a sample – but after 50 or more years, any paint will have faded. The post-war colours are simpler to deal with, and a table of present-day reference numbers appears in the colour section for the TD and TF models.

TD and TF Models

CHASSIS

The TD chassis was a completely new design compared to the TC, but was in certain respects derived from the Y-type. The prototype TD used a shortened Y-type chassis, with the wheelbase reduced from 8ft 3in to 7ft 10in (as on previous T-types). The two main side members were fully boxed in, and tapered towards the front in plan view. Between the front wheels was a substantial box section cross-member which carried the independent front suspension, the steering gear, the front engine mounting and the radiator. In addition there were three tubular cross-members – at the rear of the gearbox, at the front mounting points of the rear springs, and at the rear end of the chassis.

Unlike both the TC and the Y-type, the chassis side members were swept above the rear axle, with a reduced cross-section. After the first 100 TDs had been made, a tubular section hoop was added above the front tubular cross-member to improve scuttle stiffness. There were originally three body mounting points on each side, two on chassis outriggers below the door, the third behind the rear axle. In 1952, a fourth body mounting point was added on each side, at the foot of the scuttle hoop. The body was also attached directly to the scuttle hoop. There was a substantial pillar carrying the steering column, mounted on the left- or right-hand chassis side member depending on whether LHD or RHD was specified. The entire chassis with its attendant brackets was finished in petrol-resistant matt black paint.

The TF chassis was in all fundamental respects the same as the TD chassis, except for revised engine mounts. There were no changes to the chassis during the TF production run.

FRONT SUSPENSION

The independent front suspension on the TD had been designed by a young engineer called Alec Issigonis working for Morris Motors at Cowley before the war, and had first gone into production on the Y-type in 1947. Significantly, this particular suspension set-up was to endure with very little change until the last MGB was made in 1980. It was a straight-forward coil and wishbone lay-out. The lower wishbone was mounted in rubber-bushed bearings on the chassis. A plate between the wishbone arms carried the coil spring which at the top fitted into the inverted 'cup' formed by the ends of the front chassis cross-member where it overhung the side members. The upper wishbone was formed by the lever arms of the hydraulic shock absorber, mounted on top of the coil spring housing. Originally, Luvax Girling type PVA6X shock absorbers were used, but in 1953 a change was made to Armstrong type IS9 dampers, which were also fitted on the TF. The vertical wheel bearer which connected the outer ends of the wishbones doubled as the king pin. The camber angle was +/−1°, the castor angle was 2° and the front wheel toe-in was nil. The king pin angle was 9-10½°.

Suspension parts were generally painted black but the Armstrong shock absorbers fitted to later TDs and to TFs were left in unpainted alloy, although still with black lever arms. There were no changes to the front suspension on the TF model.

REAR SUSPENSION

Conventional semi-elliptic leaf springs continued to be used for the rear suspension, with seven leaves interleaved with rubber. The springs were mounted in rubber-bushed bearings on the outside of the chassis, the front bearings being mounted on chassis outriggers at the point of the middle tubular cross-member. These outriggers also doubled as body mounting points. At the rear end, the springs were attached to the rear chassis legs by shackles. Luvax Girling type PVA6 (and later Armstrong type DAS 10) lever arm type hydraulic shock absorbers were fitted to the outside of the chassis side members in front of the rear axle. The springs passed underneath the rear axle casing. A rebound strap was attached to each chassis side member, passing underneath the axle. There were no changes to the rear suspension during the TD/TF production run.

Reflections can be confusing. This TD front wing is in fact painted red on the underside! The suspension and steering were much the same on all TDs and TFs, but later cars had a different type of shock absorber.

Seen here on the TF, this type of handbrake was common also to the TD. Note that the edge of the carpet just behind the handbrake was bound.

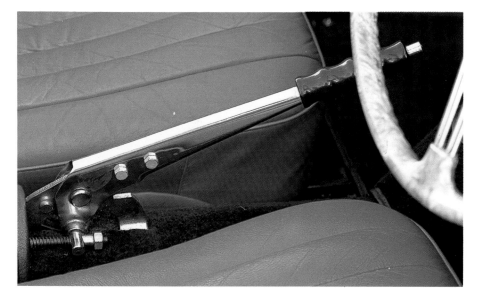

STEERING

As with the front suspension, the rack and pinion steering gear was borrowed from the Y-type. The steering rack was mounted on the front chassis cross-member, ahead of the front hubs. At either end of the rack was a short track rod. These protruded through circular holes in the chassis side members and were shrouded in rubber dust excluders.

The steering column incorporated a rubber-bushed universal joint. The column was telescopically adjustable for reach, with a clamp just below the steering wheel and a chrome-plated concertina spring covering the actual telescoping part. There was also a certain amount of adjustment for rake, on the bracket where the column was attached to the scuttle hoop. The steering column was painted black. The 16½in diameter steering wheel had three equidistantly spaced spring spokes, each spoke with four separate spring wires paired two and two. The steering wheel rim was in mottled plastic, usually light brown or bronze. The hub was painted metallic bronze and incorporated a plastic MG medallion, with silver letters and edge on a cream background, set in a dark brown surround with a chrome ring. The steering ratio was 13.75 to 1, and there were 2¾ turns lock to lock.

In October 1951, from chassis number TD/11111, the inner track rod end housing on the steering rack was changed, and in March 1953, from chassis number TD/25973, the tie rod end design was changed for a new type with improved seals. The steering gear was carried over on the TF with no further changes.

BRAKES

Another important innovation on the TD compared to the TC was that the Lockheed hydraulic brakes were now of the twin leading shoe type at the front. The drum size was 9in with linings 1½in wide. The total friction area was 99.48sq in. The linings were Ferodo MR19 on the TD, Ferodo DM7 on the TF. The combined supply tank and master cylinder was under the floor as before, directly activated by the vertically mounted brake pedal. The brake and clutch pedals shared a joint moulded rubber dust excluder, and had flat, oval, grooved pedal rubbers. Two different types of pedal arms were used on the TD. The later type had a spacer between the pedal arm and the pedal itself, and on cars fitted with this type of pedal arm, the clutch and brake pedals were also off-set rather more to the left in relation to the accelerator pedal. This allowed more space around the pedals for ease of operation.

The rear brake drums had a single cylinder, floating on the back plate, incorporating a bell-crank for handbrake operation. Two separate cables linked up with the handbrake lever, which was still of the fly-off type, but which was now mounted horizontally on the prop-shaft tunnel between the seat cushions. The lever was chrome-plated, with a black plastic grip and a chrome-plated button. The handbrake bracket was painted black and had two exposed adjusting nuts at the back.

The original brake drums were bolted and riveted to the hubs, but, from chassis number TD/4251 in November 1950, the hub and brake drum assembly became a one-piece casting. The brake drums were normally painted black. There were no further changes to the braking system during the TD/TF production run. On the wire-wheeled TF, however, different brake drums with non-integral hubs were used.

REAR AXLE

The TD was the first MG to be fitted with a hypoid bevel rear axle with semi-floating half shafts, of a standardized Nuffield design. The axle casing was in two pieces, split vertically just to the left of the centre line of the differential. The standard rear axle ratio was 5.125:1 (8/41). However, alternative rear axle ratios of 4.875:1 (8/39) and 4.55:1 (9/41) were available as optional extras. The 4.875:1 ratio was standard on the TD Mark II model (see the section on the Mark II), and was carried over on the TF models. The rear axle casing was painted black.

WHEELS AND TYRES

When the TD was introduced, it was stated that with the adoption of independent front suspension and rack and pinion steering, the steering arms and links would project so far into the plane of the wheel as to complicate the arrangement of spokes if wire wheels were used – so the TD was offered only with a deeply dished disc wheel, size 4Jx15. The wheels were attached to five studs integral with the brake drums. Originally, the wheels were plain, but in 1950 pierced wheels with 15 round ventilation holes were introduced. This supposedly happened from chassis number TD/0501 in January 1950, yet it does seem that some later cars still had the solid type of wheel. The wheels were always finished in silver paint.

The TD had chrome-plated hub caps, with an MG medallion where the background to the letters was painted red. Tyres were by Dunlop, size 5.50-15, fitted with inner tubes. A single spare wheel was fitted as standard equipment. The tubular spare wheel bracket in the form of a letter H was mounted on the chassis at the rear of the petrol tank, and attached to the rear of the body at the top. A special spare wheel carrier for two spare wheels could be obtained as an optional extra.

One modification worth listing is that from chassis number TD/12285, in December 1951, the threads on the wheel studs and nuts were changed from BSF to Unified (SAE) threads. It took until chassis number TD/12419 to change similarly the thread on the spare wheel studs and nuts!

When the TF was introduced in 1953, suddenly MG had overcome the complications of fitting wire wheels, and the TF was available with either disc or wire wheels. The disc wheels were the

same as those found on the TD, but the hub caps were now made of stainless steel and the MG medallions were left plain. The hub cap on the spare wheel had a black and white MG enamel medallion, of the same type as that fitted to the radiator (this was also found on the last TD Mark II cars – see the Mark II section).

The wire wheels were also size 4Jx15, fitted with 5.50-15 tyres. They had 48 spokes (16 outer and 32 inner) and were painted silver. They were attached by chrome-plated two-eared knock-ons with the MG logo. Wire wheels were very popular on the TF, especially in the American market, and of the 9600 TFs, 6463 cars (or 67.3%) had wire wheels. Supposedly a wire-wheeled TF should have a letter 'W' after its chassis number but I question whether this is correct for all cars. The design of the wire wheel was changed from chassis number TF/6887 in August 1954, to incorporate a deeper-dished inner flange.

TF tyre equipment was as for the TD, with some known variations on certain export models (see separate section). One car is shown in contemporary factory photographs shod with Dunlop racing tyres, but these were never quoted

Looking down the TF footwell, with a narrower baffleboard than on earlier models. The scuttle hoop can be seen on the right at the top. The pedal arms were unique to the TF but the pedal rubbers were also found on the TD. The foot-operated dipswitch was found also on later TDs. The bound carpet edges are not original, nor is the in-line fuse on the wiring.

This rather elaborate spare wheel carrier was found only on the TD. This is an export specification car and so only has the bracket for the rear number plate, rather than the backing plate found on home market cars.

right
This design of hub cap was common to both models, but this is a TF with the MG medallion left plain – on a TD it would have been filled in with a red background to the letters.

far right
By contrast, a radiator-type MG medallion was found on the spare wheel hub cap on the TF (and on the late TD Mark II models).

as official optional equipment. Whitewall tyres became available, and were in particular fitted to quite a few TF 1500s for America. Nowadays, some cars run perfectly happily on radial tyres (nearest equivalent size: 140 x 15) which are at least likely to offer increased tyre life, but with the usual penalties.

On the TF, the spare wheel carrier was a simple triangular bracket, like that fitted to the TC. A double spare wheel carrier was not quoted.

Once the TF had appeared, MG rather surreptitiously offered a 'service kit' (part number ACG 5163) to convert TDs to TF wire wheels, incorporating the hubs, wire wheels and so on from the TF, so the most legitimate wire wheeled TDs would be those that use the appropriate TF parts. Quite a number of TDs are now fitted with other proprietary wire wheels. It is still debated whether some of the last TDs were fitted with wire wheels from the factory, but I feel that it is more likely that late TDs held over in dealer stocks could have been converted before delivery to customers, which seems to have happened in the USA.

ENGINE

The XPAG engine as first employed in the TD could best be described as a cross-breed between the TC engine and the single-carburettor XPAG/SC engine used in the Y-type. MG no doubt wished to standardize components, so the TD had the rocker cover with the snap-on type oil filler at the front from the Y-type. The Y-type sump was also fitted, with the full depth of the sump carried further forward, instead of the stepped front end of the TC sump. The flywheel housing was similar to the Y-type, and so were the engine mounts and such ancillaries as the starter and dynamo. On the other hand, the twin carburettors and the hotter camshaft were inherited from the TC, and the power output of 54.4bhp was exactly the same as on the previous model.

On all TDs, the engine and gearbox were painted red, including the cylinder head, the sump, the gearbox lid and so on. The rocker cover was painted a silver grey-green colour. Ancillaries such as the starter motor, the dynamo, the air cleaner and the exhaust pipe were black. The air manifold was left in natural aluminium. The carburettor balance pipe may be either black or engine red, and the exhaust manifold was aluminized.

A small change from the start of TD production was a new combination of starter ring gear and pinion, now with 93 and 10 teeth instead of 120 and 9 teeth, which scarcely affected the gearing. The flywheel was also changed, so the flywheel and the starter ring must be kept as a pair. The major change which occurred to engine specification during the TD production run was the introduction of a bigger flywheel and an 8in diameter clutch, replacing the original 7¼in clutch, necessitating also an enlarged flywheel

The oil bath air cleaner was unique to the TD. Painting the MG octagon on the air manifold red is gilding the lily slightly! It can be seen how the right-hand radiator stay is kinked to improve access to the front carburettor jet adjusting nut, and to compensate for engine rock.

The correct colour for the rocker cover is this silver-grey. The chain for the oil filler cap would be covered with a plastic sheath on the TF. On this red TD with beige trim, the radiator slats should match the upholstery colour. The headlamps are not the correct type for the TD.

below
It is worth noting small details like this correct type of battery bar with its ordinary nut, and the correctly-painted toolbox clip. The position of the horn was changed on the TF, and, unlike this TD, most TFs did not have under-bonnet fuel pumps.

housing. This took place from engine number XPAG/TD2/9408 in July 1951. Note that the revised engine was given the distinguishing prefix XPAG/TD2; the original engine prefix had simply been XPAG/TD. It may also be noted that whereas early TD engines had the engine number plate on the flywheel housing, visible from the left as on the TC engine, later TD engines had this plate on a square plinth on the right-hand side of the crankcase, where it is also found on all TF engines. It is possible that the changed position of this plate took effect from engine number XPAG/TD2/9408. Further detail changes which took place during the TD production run will be found in the summary of changes at the end of the TD/TF section of this book.

Details of the specially tuned engine found in the TD Mark II model are described elsewhere, but it should be borne in mind that it was basically the Mark II engine specification which was adopted for the TF model in 1953, with engine type XPAG/TF. The TF therefore had the cylinder head depth reduced from 76.75mm to 75.16mm for the higher compression ratio of 8.1:1, and was fitted with the larger valves and bigger carburettors of the Mark II. Accordingly, the TF's power output matched the Mark II at 57bhp.

This was still not enough for some customers, and a year after the introduction of the TF, MG launched the TF 1500 with a 1466cc version of the XP-engine, now known as the XPEG. The increase in capacity was achieved by opening out the bore to 72mm which necessitated siamesing the front and rear pairs of cylinders respectively, losing the water space between the cylinders. The depth of the cylinder head returned to 76.75mm but the compression ratio was increased to 8.3:1, and the power output was improved to 63bhp at 5000rpm.

far right
On the ignition side of the TF engine bay we also find the separate fusebox on the bulkhead, and right at the back the new type of chassis number plate found on the TF. Note the coiling around the speedometer and rev counter cables, and how both disappear by the battery.

right
You would find the chassis and body number plates at the outer side of the toolbox on a TD. Being an export car, this car also has the 'Made in England' plate.

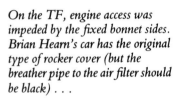

On the TF, engine access was impeded by the fixed bonnet sides. Brian Hearn's car has the original type of rocker cover (but the breather pipe to the air filter should be black) . . .

. . . while Peter Best's TF 1500 has a cast aluminium rocker cover, probably a contemporary after-market accessory. This photo shows the 'Vokes' lettering on the air cleaners, and, compared with the TD, the carburettors have shorter bodies and hexagonal tops.

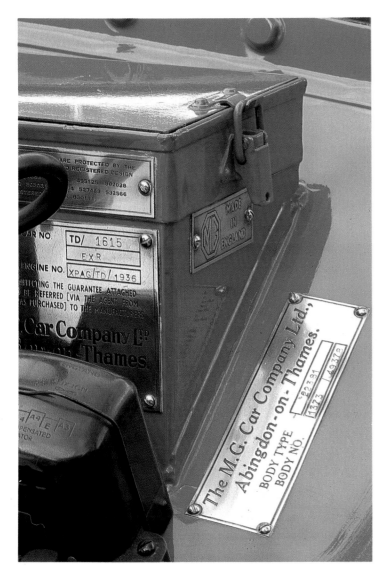

On early TDs, the valve clearance was .019in, later changed to .012in. The original plug caps were the push-on type of black bakelite.

COOLING SYSTEM

This was one area of major difference between the two models. The TD used the same cooling system as the previous T-types, but the TF had a pressurized cooling system, with an eared 4lb radiator cap under the bonnet. The octagonal cap still fitted on the outside was a sham! Another change was the introduction of a convoluted top radiator hose on the TF. Also, because the TF had a lower bonnet line, it was necessary to lower the height of the radiator core on this model, but the thickness of the core was increased to compensate. A different type of thermostat was fitted on the TF, being inset in the water outlet of the engine.

The radiator and header tank were painted black (eggshell or semi-matt) on both models. While the TD had a black four-bladed fan, some experts believe the TF had a red fan. The radiator shell was chrome-plated on both models. On the TD the radiator slats were painted. They often matched the upholstery colour, but on red or green cars with beige trim the radiator slats could be body colour. The finish on the slats was 'semi-gloss'. Late Mark II models (see the Mark II section) had chrome-plated slats. The MG badge on the TD radiator shell was brown and cream, changed on late Mark II cars to black and white. All TFs had chrome-plated slats and the black and white badge.

EXHAUST SYSTEM

On the TD, the exhaust system was rubber-mounted, so the flexible section to the front downpipe found on the TC was discontinued. The flange where the front pipe was attached to the silencer had three bolts on the TD as opposed to two bolts on the TC. On the TF the front pipe simply pushed on to the silencer inlet and was fastened with a clamp. The diameter of the tailpipe was increased on the TF model.

far left
On the TD, the uncompromisingly upright radiator was still functional, with an external filler cap of octagonal shape . . .

above
. . . whereas the TF had a radiator grille, with chrome-plated rather than painted slats.

left
The TF's external filler cap was purely cosmetic! The radiator badge was now black and white, rather than MG's traditional brown and cream.

CARBURETTORS AND FUEL SYSTEM

The carburettors were very little changed from the TC to the TD, except that the control linkage was slightly different. Otherwise they were the same SU type H2 (1¼in) slightly inclined semi-downdraught carburettors, with standard needle ES and .090in jets. A single SU electric fuel pump, type L, was mounted on the right-hand side of the front of the toolbox on the bulkhead. The air cleaner was an AC oil-bath type mounted on top of the rocker cover, this being an immediate recognition point of the under bonnet layout of the TD compared to the TC.

On the TF, the larger 1½in carburettors, type H4, from the Mark II model were used, although with shorter body castings. The TF carburettors had hexagonal brass tops without slots. Individual Vokes pancake air filters, painted black, were mounted directly on the carburettor air inlets. In February 1954, from chassis number TF/3495, piston dampers were added to the carburettor dashpots. There was apparently no change to the carburettor specification on the TF 1500 model. The standard needle for all TFs was GJ, with .090in jets.

At first the TF had a low pressure type fuel pump mounted on the scuttle similar to the TD, but from chassis number TF/1501, in December 1953, a high pressure or HP-type pump was fitted. This was mounted on the right-hand chassis side member in front of the rear wheel. Earlier cars could be modified and many probably were.

On both the TD and TF, the fuel tank was strapped to the back of the chassis in the manner of the earlier cars, but it was immediately obvious that the TD tank, compared to that of the TC, was more triangular in section, as the spare wheel was mounted at a more acute angle. Tank capacity was 12.5 imperial gallons (approximately 57 litres) of which 2.5 gallons (just over 11 litres) were 'reserve' – when the low fuel warning lamp on the dashboard would light up. The fuel tank and its retaining straps were painted body colour. The end plates were also painted body colour but were chrome-plated underneath; this showed up on the end plate edges which were left unpainted. The end plate retaining nuts were chrome-plated. The fuel filler cap on the left-hand side was in natural stainless steel, and was of the quick-release type, with an MG logo on the chrome-plated release lever. The TF fuel tank was very similar to that on the TD, but the spare wheel was angled yet further forward so the tank was again a slightly different shape.

above
The TD petrol tank may be seen in an earlier photograph. This is the rather differently shaped TF tank, with the spare wheel leaning forward at a more acute angle than on the TD. The radial tyres are strictly non-original!

The petrol filler cap was common to both models, with the MG logo on the quick-release lever. The hole is not original, and may have been drilled for a locking device.

TRANSMISSION

As on the TC, this comprised a single dry-plate Borg & Beck clutch, a four-speed gearbox (with synchromesh on the top three ratios) and a short, open Hardy-Spicer prop-shaft with universal joints. The flywheel/clutch housing and the gearbox were painted the same red as the engine, but the extension for the remote control gearlever was left in natural aluminium. The prop-shaft was painted black.

The closest relative to the TD/TF gearbox was that found on the Y-type, which had the same gearbox casing and the same internal ratios. However, the Y-type gearlever was a cranked lever coming straight out of the back of the gearbox.

The following table gives the internal and overall gear ratios for the TD and TF, the internal ratios being the same but the overall ratios being altered with the higher rear axle ratio on the TF:

	Internal ratios TD and TF	Overall ratios TD (not Mark II)	Overall ratios TF and TF 1500
First and reverse	3.50:1	17.938:1	17.063:1
Second	2.07:1	10.609:1	10.091:1
Third	1.385:1	7.098:1	6.752:1
Top	1.00:1	5.125:1	4.875:1

The Mark II overall gear ratios were in fact the same as on the TF. For all models, the overall ratios were obviously changed if one of the optional final drive ratios was fitted.

As previously mentioned, from engine number XPAG/TD2/9408 in July 1951, the clutch diameter was increased from 7¼in to 8in. In May 1952, some slight changes were made to the gearbox. From engine number XPAG/TD2/16482, a snap ring was added to the front of the top and third shift rail, and this rail was lengthened with extra support at the back of the remote control housing. From engine number XPAG/TD2/16978, a key was added to the speedometer drive worm gear. The only other transmission modification worthy of note occurred in November 1952 when the clutch operation was changed from cable to rod, at engine number XPAG/TD2/22717 and chassis number TD/22251. Also, from then on a stop bolt was added to the pedal bracket to limit clutch pedal travel.

ELECTRICAL EQUIPMENT AND LAMPS

This was all manufactured by Lucas (who else?). The single 12 volt battery, type GTW9A (GTW9A/2 on the TF), was mounted in an open battery box on the bulkhead. The box was lined with a wooden tray. The battery retaining bar was fastened with ordinary (as opposed to wing) nuts and had a rubber strip stuck on the back. It was not quite a right angle in section. Battery capacity was 51 AH. Some export cars had different batteries, and apparently there was a Police version of the TD which had not only a large capacity battery but also a bigger battery box to accommodate it. This version was also fitted with a high output dynamo and a somewhat modified wiring loom.

The electrical system was wired positive to earth. The wiring loom was insulated with rubber covered in cotton with colour coding.

The normal dynamo was type C39PV DA41 on the original TD; later TDs and TFs had a dynamo type C39PV/2. The starter motor was type M35G/1 L3/1; both this and the dynamo were painted black. The ignition coil was type Q12L on the TD and early TFs, changed to type LA12 on later TFs. Originally the TD used Champion L10S plugs with ½in reach, but from engine number XPAG/TD2/22735, in November 1952, ¾in reach Champion NA8 were specified, and these were also used on the TF. The Mark II was fitted with Champion NA10 plugs. All plugs were 14mm size and the plug gap was quoted as .020 to .022in.

The voltage regulator fitted to the early TDs was type RF95/2 with exposed fuses, similar to that fitted to the later TCs, but from chassis number TD/8142, in June 1951, it was changed to a type RB106/1 with a separate fuse box, type SF6, still with only two fuses. This was carried over on the TF.

Regardless of minor differences to suit various export markets, all TD headlamps were type S.700 with block lenses, always fitted with twin filament dipping bulbs to both lamps. The body-colour mounting brackets were similar to those used on the TC. The TD was found with both chrome-plated and painted headlamps (the latter still had chrome-plated rims). It is not possible to state specific change-over points by chassis numbers, but it can be said that the painted lamps were used owing to the chromium shortage during the Korean war – although strangely, no other chrome plating was deleted from the TD's specification! Most TD headlamps had a countersunk Lucas medallion but this was discontinued on the final chrome-plated lamps. The TF's built-in headlamps were type F.700.

The sidelamps on both models were type 1130, similar to those found on the earlier models. Originally, the TD had stop/tail lamps which were triangular or wedge-shaped when seen from the side, of the type 471 also found on the Morris Minor and other Nuffield cars. They were fitted with glass lenses which often broke, so many cars are now fitted with replacement plastic lenses of a lighter red colour, although the plastic lens was introduced only after this type of lamp had ceased

The TF headlamps were built into the front wing, but this type of lens pattern should also be found on the separately-mounted TD headlamps.

below
The sidelamps were the same on both models. This useful wing-mounted mirror is not original.

right
This was the style of rear lamp originally fitted to the TD, although on Andrew Nairne's car the original glass lenses have been replaced by later plastic lenses in a slightly lighter shade of red.

far right
Now you know why it is called the red dot!

to be fitted on the TD. From chassis number TD/21303 in 1952, round stop/tail lamps type 488 were fitted. These were mounted on a chrome-plated plinth and were also found on the TF. The number plate lamp was type 467/2 on all cars, originally with two bulbs but with only one bulb on later TD and all TF cars. It was always chrome-plated. Flashing indicators which were built into the sidelamps, and the stop/tail lamps, were found on North American specification TDs from chassis number TD/22315 in 1952, and on all TFs.

Two windtone horns were fitted, type WT614 on the TD and type WT618 on the TF. On the TD they were mounted on the bulkhead under the bonnet, the high-note horn on the right and the low-note horn on the left. On the TF they were relocated below the radiator in front of the chassis cross-member. The fog lamp was now an extra; if fitted, it was type SFT462 on the TD, and type SFT576 on the TF. It is possible that the TF could be fitted with a matching long-range driving or spot lamp of type SLR576 as an alternative (or in addition to the fog lamp).

The TD had a windscreen wiper motor type CW1 DA34 mounted on the passenger side at the top of the windscreen frame at first, but centrally from chassis number TD/22315 in 1952, thus obviating the need for changing the position of the wiper motor for LHD cars. The motor housing was finished in crackle black with a chrome-plated control. The two wiper arms and their connections were chrome-plated. By contrast, the TF had a remote wiper motor type CRT12 mounted under the bonnet, with cable drive to the wipers mounted on the scuttle below the windscreen.

Rear reflectors, type RER2, were found on all TF 1500s. They were not fitted to any TDs, or any earlier home market TFs, but may have been found on some export model TF 1250s. They were fitted to the top corners of the body, outboard of the fuel tank, on wedge-shaped rubber plinths compensating for the shape of the body.

far left
On later TDs and on this TF the rear lamp was changed to a circular type on a chrome-plated plinth.

left
This is the correct type of number plate lamp for both the TD and the TF; this is a TD, with the square number plate mounted to one side. The TF had an oblong number plate mounted centrally above the rear bumper. The silver-on-black pressed aluminium number plate is suitable for all T-types.

above
The badge bar and the fog lamp were optional on both the TD and the TF. The fog lamp fitted to Brian Hearn's TF is of a slightly too modern type for the car.

left
Reflectors were fitted from the factory on the TF 1500s, but this is the wrong position. They should be in the top corner of the body, above the rear wing outboard of the petrol tank.

BODY AND BODY TRIM

The overall impression of the TD compared to its predecessor was of a much lower, wider and squatter motor car. Obviously the smaller disc wheels with the fatter tyres contributed to this image. In fact, with the new chassis wheel tracks were wider, and the TD was also wider than the TC in terms of overall and interior width. Some 4½in were added to the width of the body in the region of the seat, so the TD was rather more comfortable than the TC.

In principle there was very little difference between the TD body and those found on the earlier models. One had to open the bonnet to appreciate one major difference – this being that the bulkhead was now always painted body colour, having been added to the body by Morris Bodies Branch at Coventry. The lidded battery box of the TC was replaced by an open battery shelf, behind which was still the toolbox, lined in cream felt and with two lids hinged in the centre. The bonnet itself followed the style of the TC but the centre bonnet hinge was now made from stainless steel.

The front valance between the chassis horns was plain without louvres. The front valance hexagonal bolts were painted body colour, but the cross-head screws were chrome-plated. The front wings came much further down in front than the TC wings. The TD running boards had three strips but the innermost strip was very short and was found only at the front, owing to the tapering shape of the running board. At the rear was a body-coloured valance which formed a shelf with a central depression for the spare wheel.

All TD and TF models were fitted with full-width chrome-plated bumpers front and rear. The bumper blade section was a simple curve, and the blades had pointed (*not* squared-off) ends. Ribbed overriders were fitted, of a type also seen on other Nuffield cars of the period. There was originally no piping between the bumpers and the overriders. The rear edge of the overrider should be flush with the rear edge of the bumper blade; some reproduction overriders are too short, in that their rear edge is forward of the edge of the bumper blade. Behind the bumper blades were full-width strengthening bars painted black, as were the brackets which were attached with ½in thick spacers to the front chassis horns on the TD. Spacers were interposed where the front bumper brackets were attached on the TF, through the front wings. At the rear, spacers were found on the bumper brackets on both models. A starting handle bracket was incorporated in the front bumper.

The badge bar of the TC was relegated to the options list. The door handles of the TD and TF were completely different from those found on earlier T-types, being of a style common to the Y-type, and fitted with a triangular escutcheon. At the rear, the TD had a square backing plate for the number plate, mounted on the driver's side of the car, with the number plate lamp above it. It was, however, often deleted on export cars, or replaced by a simpler bracket which could be adjusted to cope with different sizes of number plates.

The Auster windscreens fitted to the TD and TF were similar in design but not identical. The TF screen was raked a little further back. On both cars, the bottom of the windscreen stanchion should be flush with the panel break line on the

above
The correct type of bumper overrider sits on the bumper blade so that its rear edge is flush with the rear of the bumper blade itself, like this. On the other hand, there should strictly speaking not be any piping (fitted to prevent squeaking) between the overrider and the bumper.

top
The plain bumper bars with ribbed overriders were common to both models.

side of the scuttle. Cross-headed Philips screws were used for the first time on the TD windscreen frame. The windscreen glass was toughened on home market TDs, laminated on export cars. All TFs had laminated windscreen glass. A final point to note on both the TD and the TF is that the tread plates at the bottom of the door openings were plain, without the company name.

The TF looked radically different from the TD, although the main section of the body tub was very little changed. The front end was all new, dominated by the forward-mounted, raked radiator shell, and the bonnet line was lowered towards the front. The front wings were new, the most obvious change being that the separately mounted headlamps of the TD had been replaced by headlamps faired into the wings. The wings were also pulled down more at the front and their section was more domed.

The door handles on the TF, and the TD, lost the octagon and were of this streamlined type, also found on the Y-type saloon. The escutcheon was of a triangular shape.

far right
The front wings on the TD were pulled somewhat lower down in front than on the TC, and the bumpers were a prominent feature – although they would not withstand a determined attack from something of this size coming too close up behind.

right
On the TF, the front wings were deeper still.

left
The windscreens are very similar on the TD and TF, whether in the upright position as on this TF . . .

right
. . . or lowered, as on the TD. Both cars have cross-headed screws for the windscreen frame, and the stanchion lines up with the panel break on the side of the scuttle.

The running board was still separate. Between the wing and the running board was black rubber piping, also found at the rear of the bonnet and the bonnet side panels. Each running board had three plain chrome-plated tread strips without rubber inserts. The two outer strips were 31in long, the inner one 20½in long. The three tread strips ran well up the front wing, the inside one running furthest, with the front ends of the strips being set on a diagonal line across the wing.

The shape of the rear wings was also altered. At the front of each rear wing a flare was added to join the rear of the running board, with black rubber piping. The rear end of the rear wing was pulled further back and was raised slightly in relation to the level of the rear bumper. The void below the spare wheel was filled by a very deep shelf-like rear valance which completely filled the area between the petrol tank, the wings and the bumper.

At the front, with the radiator shell coming so much further forward, there was only the narrowest of valances behind the bumper. The TF bonnet was still of the centre-hinged two-piece type, but the bonnet sides were fixed and only the tops opened. Each bonnet side had 12 short louvres, split in two groups with three at the back and nine a little further forward. Between the louvres, and towards the front end of the bonnet side, were two chrome-plated push-button bonnet locks on each side. There was a chrome-plated trim strip to the edge of the bonnet top on each side. It may be noted that the beading found between the radiator and the wings was somewhat fatter than the ordinary wing beading.

No doubt to compensate for those fixed bonnet sides, the TF was given removable louvred aluminium panels fitted inside each front wing. They were supposed to ease access to the starter

At the rear of the TF, the valance should completely fill the void between wings, petrol tank and bumper. The gaps seen here are not correct.

motor and the oil filter (with, as one commentator put it, appropriate malediction aimed at the body designer!).

The TF rear number plate was of the oblong type, mounted centrally above the rear bumper, with the number plate lamp above it. As far as the TF 1500 was concerned, the only external recognition points were the rear reflectors previously mentioned, and small enamel badges on each side of the bonnet. They read "TF"-1500 in black letters on a white background.

The louvred detachable panels can just about be seen inside the front wing of this TF. The pattern of louvres in the fixed bonnet side was unique to this model. The single lift-the-dot fastener for the tonneau cover at the front of the door is correct.

INTERIOR TRIM AND HOOD

The TD interior (with the exception of the dashboard, and the position of the handbrake) would be immediately familiar to an owner of an earlier T-type. There was the same type of seat, with two separate cushions and a one-piece squab, and the same style of door trim panels. The carpeting, black Karvel with mostly unbound edges, was similar. However, the gearbox tunnel was now carpeted (over a steel pressing) and the exposed carpet edges behind the gearlever, and over the handbrake bracket, were bound in Rexine. There was a small plug with carpet cover, giving access to the gearbox dipstick.

Behind the seat, the heelboard was uncarpeted and painted black. The bottom of the tonneau was made from three pieces of plywood of different sizes, of which only the centre portion lifted out for access to the rear axle. On some cars it was covered in carpet fixed with press studs, on others not. As before, the floor carpet had underfelt, but this was lacking on the toeboard, which was pressed steel and was usually painted black. The gearlever had a sewn leather gaiter.

Most of the interior trim panels were in Rexine-covered plywood, but an exception was in the region of the scuttle hoop, where the panelling was in moulded fibreboard to fit around the hoop. Sometimes the front half of the sides of the footwells was covered in carpet. Under the dashboard was still the Rexine-covered scuttle masking panel or baffleboard. The starting handle was now attached to the back of the seat squab with three clips, below the tonneau cover rail.

The hood was always made from biscuit coloured single duck on the TD and TF, with the hood frame painted light tan. Originally, a two-bow hood frame similar to the TC hood frame was fitted, but from chassis number TD/20374, in 1952, a three-bow frame was fitted, and this was carried forward to the TF models. At the same time the shape of the sidescreens was changed. The early type of front sidescreen had the top of the screen sloping down towards the rear. With the three-bow frame, the top and bottom lines of the celluloid in the sidescreen were parallel, and the top line of the rear sidescreen was at a steeper angle. Because of the steeper rake of the windscreen, the TF sidescreens were different from those on the TD. There was a small patent number plate at the top inside the front sidescreens. The hood cover had a single rear window measuring approximately 8in by 24in.

The usual half tonneau cover, tucking over the black-painted tonneau rail at the back of the seat, was standard on the TD. It is likely that the full length tonneau cover was offered as an optional extra but I have not actually been able to document this to my satisfaction. The compartment was lined in black felt. The sidescreens were still stored in a vertical compartment at the back of the tonneau, as on the TC and earlier models.

Inside the TF, the most important change from the TD was that two individual bucket type seats were now fitted. They were individually adjustable with a lever at the bottom outside front corner of each seat cushion. The seat frames were

above
The felt lining in the toolbox on Peter Best's TF looks remarkably clean! Only on this model would you find the body number plate on the inside of the toolbox lid. The battery is none too easy to get at or remove on a T-type with an under-bonnet mounted battery.. The push-button activated bonnet lock can be clearly seen.

right
About the only distinguishing mark of the TF 1500 was this discreet badge found on each side of the bonnet, just behind the front bonnet lock.

far left
The TD interior was typical of the MG Midget, with individual cushions and a one-piece seat squab. This is the early TD two-bow hood, and the hood frame and sidescreen frames are painted the correct tan colour. The door sill tread plates should correctly be plain, without lettering.

left
With the hood up and the sidescreens in place, the front edge of the sidescreen should be parallel with the windscreen stanchion. On the TF the wipers were mounted on the scuttle, with cable drive from a remote wiper motor under the bonnet.

below
On the TD, the starting handle was clipped to the back of the seat squab. The tonneau rail is painted the correct black, and the method of adjusting the squab angle with a quadrant each side can be seen clearly. The carpet to the floor of the luggage area in the tonneau is correct on the TD.

hinged to the floor at the front so that the seats could be tilted forward. The tonneau rails (which were now painted tan) on the backs of the seats doubled as convenient grab handles for this purpose. The wearing surfaces and the edges of the cushions were upholstered in leather, with the edges and the backs of the squabs in Rexine. The stitching pattern had seven flutes to each squab but only six to the cushion, in each case with border panels which were rather wider than the individual flutes.

Behind the seats, the sidescreens of the TF were stored in a horizontal compartment in the floor of the tonneau. This was lined with black felt and had a Rexine-covered lid hinged at the back. Other

above
At the rear of the door, the sidescreen was located with a peg in this hole. The front mounting point for the rear sidescreen was similar to that at the front of the door. Door hinges were always body-coloured.

top
The style of door trim on the TF did not differ greatly from earlier models. Common to TD and TF was the triangular backing plate for the sidescreen mounting point.

top right
The front sidescreens had a stiffener sandwiched between two layers of material, and the chrome-plated beading round the celluloid windows bolted on to the frames on the inside. (It is not to be wondered that people often describe the MG Red as 'Pillarbox Red'!) The key-operated external door lock is not original.

right
This is the distinctive shape of the sidescreens for the early TD two-bow hood. This is the correct material and colour for the hood, without contrast-colour piping.

left
The TF interior was fundamentally altered with the new individual seats. The revised sidescreens, introduced with the three-bow hood on later TDs, had the top and bottom of the celluloid in the front sidescreen parallel. Note the strap for attaching the sidescreen flap to the press stud on the door trim, and the patent number plate at the top of the front sidescreen.

right
There was no significant change to the TF hood cover. Note how the overlap in material across the back of the hood disappears into the seam over the top rear corner of the sidescreen.

below right
The TF hood tucks away quite neatly when it is fully down, and could be covered with the half-tonneau cover supplied as standard with the car. Even with this tonneau cover in place, both front and rear sidescreens could be erected.

small changes on the TF concerned the position of the starting handle, which was now clipped to the rear body panel at the back of the tonneau, and the heelboard which was now covered in carpet. Finally, the under-dash masking panel did not now extend to the full width of the scuttle.

When the TF was discussed by the assembled panel of experts in preparation for this book, it was felt that at some time during the model's production run a change was made from the old Rexine trim material to the then new Vynide (PVC) material. Unfortunately, there are no part number changes in the Service Parts List to document this, and the body material specification is singularly unhelpful. It may in fact be that Vynide was used right from the start of TF production.

The hood cover of the TD followed the pattern of the late TC models, with a rear window which at the time was considered to be very adequate.

above
Peter Best's TF is fitted with the optional full-length tonneau cover which obviously cannot be used with the sidescreens in place. This tonneau cover requires additional lift-the-dot fasteners on the rear quarter panels, the doors and the scuttle (one on each side, and one on each side of the mirror) . . .

right
. . . some of which can be seen in this photograph, which also shows the relative positions of the running board tread strips, which are plated without rubber inserts.

far left
Partly folded, the TF hood reveals the relative simplicity of the construction of the hood frame.

The TF seats tilt forward for easy access to the tonneau, and the sidescreen storage compartment is now in the floor rather than at the back. The lining was black felt and the top of the lid was covered in Rexine to match the other interior trim panels. The heelboard was now carpeted. The tonneau rails on the seat backs should be painted tan or beige.

The Rexine-covered dashboard of the TD echoes the TC dashboard in shape but the layout was changed, with both major instruments now in front of the driver. The ash tray is not original. This type of ash tray is a period Nuffield item, found on Morris Minors and Wolseleys. The direction indicator switch below the centre of the dashboard is another period style non-original fitting.

What MG instrument lighting is all about!

DASHBOARD AND INSTRUMENTS (TD)

As this is one area where the TD and TF models were completely different, I will consider the two cars separately. The TD dashboard was similar in shape to the TC, and, like the later TC dashboards, it was made from plywood covered in Rexine to match the upholstery colour. The layout was completely changed, with both of the main instruments now in front of the driver, and a glovebox in front of the passenger. The dashboards on RHD and LHD cars were complete mirror images. Thus the speedometer was always towards the outside of the car and the rev counter towards the centre, and similarly the positions of minor gauges and switches on the central penel were reversed on LHD cars.

Looking at a RHD car, starting from the right (which would be starting from the left on a LHD car), the speedometer read to 105mph and incorporated a five-figure total odometer as well as a three-figure and decimal trip meter, with a re-set button under the dashboard. The rev counter read to 6500rpm and incorporated an electric clock. The instruments had silver grey-green dials and brown figures and pointers. The early TD instruments were of the chronometric type with flat dials, similar to those found on the TC, but from chassis number TD/10751, in October 1951, they were replaced by magnetic instruments with a flat centre and a dished outer circle to the dial. The instruments were made by Jaeger. Some variation did occur to the colour of the dials. The traditional green rim lighting was still used.

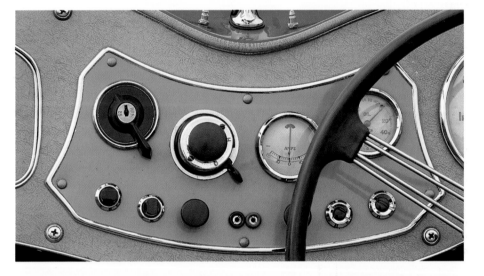

The central instrument panel was very similar to that of the TC. It was chrome-plated but this showed only on the edge, with the centre of the panel painted in the same metallic bronze colour which was used on the steering wheel hub. Again, looking from right to left (or the other way on a LHD car), the first instrument was a Jaeger oil pressure gauge with its pointer sweeping clockwise to 160lb/sq in. On cars from chassis number TD/13914, this gauge was replaced by a combined oil pressure gauge and water temperature gauge (previously quoted as an optional extra). Next to this was a Lucas ammeter, originally reading to +/− 20 amp, but from chassis number TD/10751 it was replaced by a +/− 30 amp gauge. The design and colour of the two smaller gauges followed the larger ones.

Next to the ammeter was a combined horn push and dip switch, on a black bezel with white lettering. In August 1952, from chassis number TD/18883, this was replaced by just a horn push, as the dip switch was changed to a foot-operated type, mounted to the left and above the clutch pedal. Last in the top row on the instrument panel was the combined ignition lock and light switch, its black bezel lettered OFF-S-H. The ignition key number (in the MRN range) was stamped on the front of the lock barrel.

In the bottom row on the panel, from right to left on a RHD car, was a red ignition warning lamp, followed by a green warning lamp for low fuel level (2.5 imperial gallons). Then there was the pull-operated starter, an inspection lamp socket, the choke pull, a switch for fog lamp(s) if fitted, and lastly the panel light switch. This was originally a simple on/off switch, but from chassis number TD/10751 it was changed to a rheostat type switch. There was no indication of the functions of the knobs and switches.

On North American export TDs from chassis number TD/22315, in December 1952, there was an additional control in the shape of a switch for the flashing direction indicators, this being a self-cancelling switch of the dashpot or air valve type mounted under the dashboard on the driver's side. These cars also had a warning lamp mounted centrally on the instrument panel, the hole for which was covered by a blanking plug on cars not fitted with direction indicators.

In front of the passenger, the glovebox was made from flock-sprayed cardboard. The inside and outside of the lid were covered in Rexine matching the dashboard, the lid having chrome-plated beading and an octagonal bakelite knob. The lid hinges were also chrome-plated. The factory fitted radio, an HMV or a Radiomobile valve unit, had its control unit installed in the glovebox.

All the instruments had chrome-plated edges. There was chrome-plated beading around the whole dashboard panel, and Rexine-covered rubber piping around the top of the panel where it butted up to the scuttle. This piping continued down to the door lock and further down following the front edge of the door on either side. The rear view mirror was mounted centrally on the top of the scuttle, and had a chrome-plated back and stem.

DASHBOARD AND INSTRUMENTS (TF)

Where the earlier models had the dashboard set flush with the edge of the scuttle, on the TF the dashboard was set well back under the scuttle, at an angle to facilitate the reading of the instruments. The rear top edge of the scuttle was finished with a strip of foam padding covered in leathercloth to match the upholstery colour. The dashboard itself was in painted metal, red on cars with red or biscuit trim, green on cars with green trim. The two open gloveboxes in front of the driver and passenger were made from millboard, lined with leathercloth to match the upholstery.

In the centre was the instrument panel, painted metallic bronze with chrome-plated beading. There were three instrument dials, octagonal in shape; the dials were black with white figures and pointers, and were set in chrome-plated bezels. The instruments were similar to those found on the Y-type saloons, but were not the same. The positions of the speedometer and rev counter were changed over on a LHD car.

Looking at a RHD car from left to right, first came a 105mph speedometer, with the trip meter now above and the total odometer below, and an electric clock inset at the bottom. In the centre was a combination dial, with a water temperature gauge on top left reading to 110° C, an oil pressure gauge on top right reading to 100lb/sq in, and an ammeter at the bottom, reading to +/− 30 amp. Nearest to the driver was a rev counter marked to 6500rpm (still no red line), with a main beam warning lamp at the bottom of the dial. The instruments were by Jaeger, except for the Lucas ammeter.

Above the instruments was, in the left corner, a panel light switch marked P which in its second position switched on two map reading lamps, mounted under the scuttle in front of the driver and passenger. In the centre were three warning lamps – blue for low fuel level, red for the ignition, and green for direction indicators. In the top right corner was a switch marked A for auxiliary, which could be used for fog lamp(s) if fitted. Below the

below left
The TD instrument panel is superficially like that of the TC but the sequence of instruments and controls was altered. Also unlike earlier models, the individual knobs and switches were not labelled. The bezel for the light switch should be lettered 'OFF-S-H'. The horn button surround should be black with white letters.

bottom left
Some experts feel that a brown mottled steering wheel rim would be more correct, and mottled ivory steering wheels may also be found – perhaps especially on American export models. The instrument dials should be the same colour but were often slightly mis-matched. On this car the speedometer may be from a slightly later car. These early TD instruments were very much like the TC instruments in design.

below
The TF dashboard was completely changed from the earlier models. Octagonal instruments were also found on the Y-type saloons of the period. Red dashboards were found on TFs with red or biscuit trim, but TFs with green trim had green dashboards.

instruments were the choke pull marked C, a two-stage light switch marked L, the ignition lock (with FA key numbers), and the starter pull marked S. The five knobs and switches were octagonal, coloured black with white letters, and set in chrome-plated bezels. On LHD cars, the choke and starter controls changed places.

There was a knurled knob for the wipers in each glovebox, that on the driver's side being the master switch for the electric motor, and that on the passenger side merely connecting the wiper on that side to the drive mechanism. The horn push was on the driver's right (left on a LHD car) under the scuttle, and the self-cancelling direction indicator switch at the end of the dashboard just below this. The matching hole at the opposite end

of the dashboard was covered with an MG medallion. The dip switch was foot-operated. There was a chrome-plated grab handle under the scuttle on the passenger side. The rear view mirror, also chrome-plated, was mounted centrally on the top of the scuttle.

If a radio was fitted, the control unit occupied the glovebox in front of the passenger, as on the TD. A heater was never fitted as standard on the TF, but certain heaters were approved for installation (see list of optional extras at the end of this section), and at least two cars were fitted with heaters by the factory.

EXPORT VARIATIONS

In the TD/TF range there was no such distinctive model as the TC/EX-U. Rather, the different export models were permutations of a number of specification differences. Most obvious was whether a car had right- or left-hand drive, and a miles-per-hour or kilometres-per-hour speedometer. As previously mentioned, the LHD TDs had a mirror-image dashboard, while on a LHD TF merely the main instruments were changed over.

Another permutation depended on the type of headlamps fitted. Basically all of these cars had S.700 or F.700 headlamps (TD and TF respectively) but they were supplied in different versions to suit different markets, as follows:

RHD cars, home and export: dip to the left
RHD cars for countries driving on the right: dip vertically
LHD cars, except North America and France: dip vertically
LHD cars for North America: dip to the right
LHD for France: dip vertically or to the right, special yellow glass

Furthermore, there is evidence that some cars for the USA were supplied without the actual headlamp units but with empty shells for local fitting of sealed beam units. Sealed beam

above left
The only differences on a left-hand drive car would be that the positions of the speedometer and the rev counter were changed over, as were the starter and choke controls.

above
The MG medallion at the end of the dashboard hides the hole where the direction indicator switch was found on a left-hand drive TF. The design of the door lock hardly changed on the T Series cars. The triangular backing plate for the sidescreen mounting point was characteristic of the TD and TF models. This is the correct type of grab handle on the TF.

left
The same metallic tan or bronze colour was used on the instrument panel and the steering wheel hub. The steering wheel with the plastic MG medallion was common to both TD and TF. Even the knobs and switches were octagonal on the TF!

headlamps and turn signals were required by law on new cars in many American states from 1952, if not earlier, and to comply MG cars might have had to be modified by local dealers prior to sale. Later North American TDs and all TFs had flashing indicators fitted from the factory.

Some export cars were supplied with a different battery, Lucas type GTZ9A/1 or GTZ9A/2, which was dry-charged from the factory. On cars to certain destinations (Australia, New Zealand) and on CKD cars, a battery was usually not fitted.

Reinforced six-ply tyres were found on cars supplied to African markets, and Dunlop 'Green Label' tyres were fitted to cars for certain European markets. Again on cars to Australia, New Zealand and on CKD cars, tyres and tubes were usually not supplied.

The rear number plate and lamp were mounted on the left on a LHD TD, but the number plate was often deleted or replaced by a bracket on export cars. Also as mentioned previously, export TDs had laminated windscreens whereas home market cars had toughened windscreens. Cars for France had a special type of laminated glass. Finally, rear reflectors may have been fitted to some export cars before they became standard on all cars, from the start of the TF 1500 model.

TD MARK II OR TD/C MODEL

The first tuned competition TD (registered FMO 885) was built in early 1950 and was given to Dick Jacobs to race. This car incorporated all of the features that we now associate with the Mark II model, but also had lightweight bucket seats which were not part of the normal Mark II specification. A genuine Mark II model can be identified by its chassis number prefix, TD/C, and on later cars from engine number 17029, in June 1952, by the engine number prefix, which then became XPAG/TD3.

The production Mark II had its engine tuned to give 57–61bhp, more or less as to Special Tuning Stage 1/1A. The cylinder head was machined from the standard depth of 76.75mm to 74.37mm, which increased the compression ratio from 7.25 to 8.6:1. The valve diameter was increased by 3mm – inlet from 33 to 36mm, exhaust from 31 to 34mm. Stronger valve springs were fitted. The 1¼in carburettors were replaced by H4 1½in carburettors, the intake manifold was bigger, and a larger air cleaner was fitted. Later Mark II cars had a different distributor with a revised advance curve. Some cars were fitted with a sports ignition coil, and all Mark IIs had two fuel pumps, the

second one mounted on the outer side of the toolbox, slightly behind the standard fuel pump. A manual ignition advance/retard control was fitted.

As far as the chassis was concerned, the final drive ratio was raised from 5.125:1 to 4.875:1, and in addition to the normal hydraulic shock absorbers, adjustable Andrex friction shock absorbers were fitted front and rear.

There were originally no body modifications, but from chassis number TD/C/22613, in December 1952, the Mark II was given enamel badges reading 'Mark II' on either side of the bonnet and on the rear bumper. To distinguish the car from the standard model, Mark II models were now given chrome-plated radiator slats (they stayed painted on the ordinary TD), and the MG badge on the radiator nosepiece was changed (again only on Mark IIs) from brown and cream to black and white. A radiator type badge was now fitted also to the hub cap of the spare wheel of the Mark IIs. Some of the later Mark II models for export may have had reflectors fitted on the rear bumper.

Further changes at this time included a reduced compression ratio of 8.1:1, with the cylinder head depth now being 75.16mm. This was the cylinder head carried forward on the TF model. The air intake manifold was enlarged, and a small bulge was added to the right-hand bonnet side panel for clearance. A tubular section grab handle was mounted under the dashboard on the passenger side.

The same optional extras were available on the Mark II as on the standard TD, including the even higher final drive ratio of 4.55:1, and the engine could obviously be tuned even further by the various Stages described by the factory. At least one car was fitted with a supercharger from the factory.

The first production Mark II was a right-hand drive export car built in May 1950 with chassis number TD/C/1123. Only a few more cars were built in this year, although they included the three works racing cars (registered FRX 941, FRX 942 and FRX 943) which were raced at Silverstone and in the TT by Dick Jacobs, George Phillips and Ted Lund. Mark II production was only increased to substantial levels when MG began making them for the American export market in January 1951.

Various figures have previously been quoted for Mark II production, in particular a total figure of 1022 cars, but research recently carried out by the author using the TD guarantee plate issue ledgers kept in the MG Car Club archive has revealed that 1710 cars can be identified as Mark II models through being listed with the TD/C chassis prefix in these records. Also for the first time, on the left is a breakdown of Mark II production – compare this with the total TD production and export figures found elsewhere in this book. Regrettably there is no indication of the destination of the two left-hand drive chassis.

Of the revised Mark II model made from December 1952 onwards, there were 315 cars. The last Mark II was chassis number TD/C/29909, a North American LHD export car, which is thought to be still in existence. This was built on the last day of TD production, 17 August 1953.

	1950	1951	1952	1953	Total, all years
Home market	4	0	2	45	51
Export, RHD	24	11	4	12	51
Export, LHD	2	0	0	11	13
Export, North America	0	459	977	157	1593
Chassis only, LHD	1	0	0	1	2
All specifications	31	470	983	226	1710

It should be pointed out that the original Jacobs car, FMO 885, is unlikely to be included in the statistics above, which are based only on production cars. Another Mark II not included would be George Phillips' streamlined 1951 Le Mans car, registered UMG 400.

THE ARNOLT-MG

The romantic version of the Arnolt story goes as follows. Once upon a time there was an Italian coachbuilder called Bertone. His company was in a bad way and he was at his wits' end to drum up business. Somehow he managed to buy – cheaply, one imagines – two chassis from one of those small English sports cars. By burning the midnight oil and staving off the creditors, Bertone got two bodies – a coupé and a convertible – built on these chassis which happened to be MG TDs, and he hired a stand at the Turin Motor Show in April 1952 to show them off.

On to Bertone's stand walked a gigantic American in a cowboy outfit. He said he wanted to buy the cars. An astounded Bertone could not believe his luck; the American wanted to buy *both* cars? No, said the American, who happened to be 'Wacky' Arnolt, the ebullient Nuffield distributor from Chicago – he wanted a hundred cars of each type. A deal was struck, and Bertone was back in business.

The two show cars were shipped to the USA, and Arnolt persuaded MG at Abingdon to lay on a supply of chassis. From November 1952 to May 1953 a total of 100 chassis was sent to Turin, where they were finished with hand-made coachwork – 65 coupés and 35 convertibles. The cars were then shipped to Arnolt in Chicago. Unfortunately for 'Wacky', they proved rather difficult to sell, and he did not shift the last few cars before 1958 or 1959. The reason for this was that the Arnolt-MG cost $3145 (with disc wheels, less extras) when it was launched in New York in April 1953 at a time when the standard TD cost $2157 and a Jaguar XK120 less than $4000.

The Bertone bodies were made from steel, with doors, bonnet and boot lid in aluminium. They were 2+2 seaters with a generous boot. The styling was straightforward early 1950s Italian, with a traditional MG radiator grille incorporated. The chassis were supplied from MG with a complete set of instruments which were installed in front of the driver, speedometer and rev counter on each side with the instrument and switch panel directly above the steering column, mounted upside down!

Many Arnolt cars were fitted with Borrani or Dunlop wire wheels, and other options included heater, radio, a fresh-air ventilation system, a badge bar, as well as cast aluminium rocker and tappet covers, both made by the Arnolt corporation. Some of the later cars were fitted with 1466cc XPEG (TF 1500) engines, taken from Arnolt's store of service parts.

At least 50 of the 102 Arnolt-MGs are known to survive, and as this was being written in early 1989, when the strength of the Pound against the Dollar had made it big business to re-import British sports cars from the USA, it is interesting to note that two Arnolt coupés have found their way 'back' to Britain.

ENGINE TUNING (XPAG/XPEG)

In 1949, the MG company first issued the Special Tuning booklet for the XPAG engine. Later issues were updated so that precise instructions were available for all models, including the XPEG engine in the TF 1500. While it is unlikely that many owners of road-going cars will now wish to tune their engines, it is worth giving a brief account of the various stages of tuning which could be said to be part of the original specification of the T Series cars.

Although MG would happily sell you the necessary parts, the company was at pains to stress that they could not supply new cars in tuned form, nor would they undertake to tune owners' cars. Customers were warned that super-tuning as

92

described in the booklet would invalidate the guarantee on a new car, and that here, as elsewhere, 'Power Costs Money'. It must also be remembered that the original tuning booklets were written at a time when the only fuel available was 'pool' petrol of 70 or (with luck!) 80 octane rating, so all sorts of weird and wonderful fuel mixtures were recommended which we can forget about these days. Or does someone fancy having a go at running a supercharged TD on *lead-free* 80 octane aviation fuel? They claimed it was possible.

Stage 1 was fairly simple. It called for an increased compression ratio of 8.6:1 which meant machining the cylinder head, by various amounts depending on model. TB, TC and TD heads were reduced from 76.75 to 74.37mm; TF 1250 heads from 75.16 to 74.37mm; and TF 1500 heads from 76.75 to 76.25mm. The head, the ports and the manifold were polished, otherwise the engine was left more or less as standard. A Stage 1 XPAG engine should give 60–61bhp, and the XPEG engine 65bhp.

An additional Stage 1A applied to the TB, TC and TD models. The compression ratio was again raised to 8.6:1 but Mark II size valves were fitted. By using special sodium-cooled exhaust valves, the engine could still be run on 70 octane fuel. With 1½in carburettors (needle LS1) and a Lucas BR12 sports ignition coil, around 61bhp could be expected.

Stage 2 involved machining the cylinder head down to 73.575mm, the minimum depth recommended for all XPAG 1250cc engines. On the TF 1500 XPEG engine the finished depth should be 75.50mm. In all cases, this would raise the compression ratio to 9.3:1. On TD and earlier engines, the larger valves were fitted. With Champion LA11 plugs, power output should be 63–64bhp, and if 1½in carburettors were fitted this should improve to 66–68bhp. For TF models already fitted with the larger valves and 1½in carburettors, 64bhp could be expected, and 67bhp from a TF 1500.

With Stage 3, we enter the world of racing. This involved fitting TD and earlier engines with special pistons, in conjunction with a standard cylinder head, for a compression ratio of 12:1. With standard 1¼in carburettors (0.100in jets and GK needles), LA14 racing plugs and ignition retarded to 4° ATDC, the result should be 73bhp. The use of a competition cylinder head gasket and the dual fuel pump set-up was recommended. If in addition larger valves were fitted, power should be 76bhp. With 1½in carburettors (0.125in jets and VE needles), 80bhp should be available; and with VJ needles, running on pure alcohol, 83bhp was within reach.

For the TF (1250cc), Stage 3 involved the 9.3:1 compression ratio and a semi-racing camshaft (part no AEG 122); with few other modifications, this should yield 66bhp. For the TF 1500, this camshaft should be used together with a 9.45:1 compression ratio (machining the cylinder head down to 75.16mm) The result should be 70bhp. On Stage 3 tuned TF engines, the oil pressure should be increased to 80lb/sq in and a special distributor fitted.

Stages 4 and 5 of TB/TC/TD engine tuning both called for the installation of a Shorrock (or Nordec) supercharger, belt-driven from the crankshaft pulley. With a single 1½in carburettor, 69 to 75bhp could be expected depending on the fuel used. In Stage 5, the supercharger installation was combined with the 9.3:1 compression ratio and the larger valves, resulting in 88bhp – or, if using a 1¾in H6 carburettor, up to 97bhp.

The supercharger installation was not quoted for the TF, but TF Stage 4 tuning involved the additional fitting of a four-pipe exhaust system, and, for 1500 engines, a high overlap racing camshaft (part no. 168551). The compression ratio was increased to 10.7:1 by machining the cylinder head to a finished depth of 73.575mm (the minimum recommended depth also for the XPEG engine). With either 1½in or 1¾in carburettors, 79 or 82bhp were within reach.

The parts required to carry out the various stages of tuning were available from MG's service department, as were a range of Champion and Lodge plugs suitable for racing, the Lucas high-performance BR12 ignition coil, and even a Lucas 4 V.R.A. vertical magneto suitable for XPAG/XPEG engines. Other useful gadgets are quoted in the list of optional extras for the TD model, but they could obviously equally easily be fitted to other T Series cars. It may be noted that wider wheels of 16in diameter were available for TB and TC models.

The enthusiast who wishes to know more should consult MG's Special Tuning booklets: L/8 (with supplement L/8/1) for early XPAG engines; L/10 for the XPAG/TD engines; and L/17 for the XPAG/TF and XPEG engines. Articles in *The Autocar* for 18 and 25 July 1952 and by Eric Blower in the Nuffield magazine *Motoring* for July and August 1957 are useful. The same Eric Blower put this information in his famed MG Workshop Manual as well.

IDENTIFICATION AND DATING (TD)

A TD chassis number is prefixed with the letters TD, or TD/C on the Mark II model. Two TD prototypes had chassis numbers TD/0250 and TD/0251. The first production car was TD/0252, and the chassis number series ran to TD/29915, which equals 29,664 cars made (compare the production figure table which follows). The maker's guarantee plate was fixed on the left-hand side on the front of the toolbox. There was space below the chassis number for a code used only on export cars. The different codes found here may be interpreted as follows:

EX-R	Export car with right-hand drive and mph speedometer
EX-RK	Export car with right-hand drive and kph speedometer
EX-L	Export car with left-hand drive and kph speedometer
EX-LM	Export car with left-hand drive and mph speedometer
EX-U	Export car to North American specification (to March 1950)

From March 1950 to approximately August 1951, the following codes were used on North American cars:

EX-L-U   North American export car with left-hand drive

EX-R-U   North American export car with right-hand drive

From approximately May 1951 on some cars, and from August 1951 on all cars, the North American codes were changed to the following:

EX-L-NA   North American export car with left-hand drive

EX-R-NA   North American export car with right-hand drive

North American cars were usually fitted with an mph speedometer, but if a kph speedometer was fitted (for export to Mexico) the code may have been amended to EX-L-NA-K.

The engine number was also stamped on the guarantee plate. In addition, it was found on an octagonal plate on the engine itself, originally fixed to the left-hand side of the flywheel bell housing, later moved to the right-hand side of the crankcase. The engine number series began with 501 and ran to at least 30287. The following engine number prefixes may be found:

XPAG/TD   Engine numbers from 501 to 9407, with 7¼in clutch

XPAG/TD2   Engine numbers from 9408 upwards, with 8in clutch

XPAG/TD3   Mark II engines only, from engine number 17029 upwards (earlier Mark II engines had standard prefixes)

In addition, engines on left-hand drive cars to approximately February 1952 had the letters LHX following the engine prefixes quoted above. The LHX code seems to have been dropped on later engines, and no such code is found in the engine number of any right-hand drive car.

Each car also had a body number plate, on the left-hand side of the bulkhead by the toolbox. This quoted the body type number, the body number itself and the body batch number. No records of the TD body numbers exist and the numbers found on individual cars would be difficult to make sense of, without much further research. A typical body number plate reads as follows:

Body type   22381
Body number   1373/49378

This particular plate is from Andrew Nairne's early 1950 car, and it is thought that the first set of figures in the lower line (1373) is the actual body number. The body type number 22381 may be common to all TDs.

On the left-hand end of the toolbox on export cars was another plate with the MG badge and the legend 'Made in England' (similar to TC export cars). This plate was deemed superfluous as far as home market cars were concerned! Finally there was a plate quoting patent numbers above the maker's guarantee plate.

An approximate guide to dating a TD is given by the following list of the first chassis numbers issued in each year, taken from the guarantee plate issue ledgers. For this reason, these numbers do not quite match the annual production figures (compare the table which follows.

Nov. 1949	TD/0252 (first production TD)
Jan. 1950	TD/0349
Jan. 1951	TD/5170
Jan. 1952	TD/12578
Jan. 1953	TD/23635
Aug. 1953	TD/29915 (the last TD)

Apart from on the guarantee plate, the chassis number should also be stamped in the chassis frame itself, on the vertical outside surface of the left-hand front chassis horn which carries the front bumper, but usually hidden by the front wing and valance.

IDENTIFICATION AND DATING (TF)

In April 1952, on Morris and Wolseley cars built at Cowley, the new unified Nuffield car number prefix system was brought into use. Abingdon did not catch up with this system before the autumn of 1953, when it was introduced on the TF, the MG Magnette ZA and the Riley Pathfinder, which were then going into production. The Nuffield car or chassis number system prescribed a five character alpha-numeric prefix of three letters and two numbers. The series of numbers for each model began with 501 which was the traditional starting number for Wolseley and later Morris cars, in the same way that MG's starting number was 251. It may be noted that the Wolseley factory's telephone number in Birmingham was East 1501!

The maker's guarantee plate on the TF was found on the left-hand side of the bulkhead at the end of the toolbox and quotes both the chassis number (or car number) and the engine number. A TF chassis number prefix would normally start with the letters HD, H for MG Midget, D for open two-seater bodywork. These were followed by a third letter which indicated the paint colour and may be decoded as follows:

A – Black
B – Light Grey (Birch Grey)
C – Red (MG Red)
E – Green (MG Green, or Almond Green)
H – CKD finish (primer), found on CKD cars
P – Ivory

Next was a number which indicated the specification class, as follows:

1 – right-hand drive home market cars
2 – right-hand drive export cars
3 – left-hand drive export cars
4 – North American export cars, usually with left-hand drive
5 – CKD cars with right-hand drive
6 – CKD cars with left-hand drive

The final number in the prefix indicated the paint finish, and the following may be found on a TF:

3 – all-cellulose paint finish (normal on green TFs)

5 – primer finish, found on CKD cars

6 – cellulose finish on body, and synthetic finish on wings (normal on TFs in all colours other than green)

A number '4' would indicate metallic paint finish, but although some TFs were finished in Metallic Green, these still had the figure '3' in the prefix.

Typical code examples would be HDE 13 (a green home market car) or HDC 46 (a red North American car). One car that did not have the normal prefix was a home market TF delivered in chassis-only form which simply had a prefix HK 1, the 'K' indicating chassis form, and of course the letter and number for the paint were deleted. The TF chassis number prefix system has sometimes erroneously been referred to as the BMC system. In fact, the very different BMC system was introduced later, and first appeared on MG cars in 1959.

The prototype TF was given chassis number TF/0250; this is Peter Best's car registered KBL 296 and photographed for this book (it was later rebuilt by MG as the TF 1500 prototype). A pre-production car with chassis number TF/0251 is also still in existence. Production cars, however, started from chassis number 501 and continued to 10100, so 9600 cars were made.

The engine number stamped on the guarantee plate was repeated on the octagonal plate on the right-hand side of the crankcase. The TF 1250 engine prefix was XPAG/TF; the engine number series continued from the TD engine numbers, starting with 30301 and running to at least 36516. On the TF 1500, the engine number prefix was XPEG, and these numbers ran from 501 to at least 3936.

On the body number plate, the body type was described simply as TF. Again no records exist of the body numbers, but they seem to be around 10,000 higher than the chassis numbers. The body plate was found on the inside of the left-hand tool-box lid. A patent number plate was found near the guarantee plate. On the TF, the chassis number was stamped in the frame in the same place as on the TD. Here it will be prefixed simply 'TF', if at all.

The following list of first chassis numbers by year is, like the previous similar lists in this book, taken from the guarantee plate issue ledgers and is therefore no more than an approximate guide. For exact production figures, please see the table in the following section.

September 1953	501	(first production TF)
January 1954	2178	
July 1954	6501	(the first TF 1500)
September 1954	6950	(the last TF 1250)
January 1955	8644	
April 1955	10100	(the last TF)

From July to September 1954, the two models were produced side by side. The following batches of chassis numbers were allocated to TF 1500 models: 6501-6650, 150 cars; 6751-6850, 100 cars; 6951-10100, 3150 cars. The total number of TF 1500 cars was thus 3400, leaving 6200 TF 1250 cars.

OPTIONAL EXTRAS (TD)

External mirror, Desmo no.44P1, with convex glass and double-jointed arm.

Luggage carrier (the external mirror was always supplied when a luggage carrier was fitted).

Double spare wheel carrier. Two types, depending on whether a luggage carrier was fitted or not. With distance piece if competition tyres were fitted.

Competition tyres, 6.00-15 Dunlop Fort, on 4.50 Jx15 wheels.

Badge bar and fog lamp mounting (two mounting brackets for lamps).

Lucas type SFT462 fog lamp.

Shock absorbers with special low setting, or double hydraulic shock absorbers.

Additional Andrex friction shock absorbers (standard on Mark II model).

Alternative rear axle ratios, 4.875:1 (8/39) (standard on Mark II) or 4.55:1 (9/41).

Tow bar attachment (max towing capacity: 15cwt or 763kg).

Combined oil pressure gauge and water temperature gauge (standard from TD/13914).

Oil thermometer.

Competition clutch (for 7¼in or 8in clutches).

Manual ignition control (usually fitted on Mark II).

Radio, usually a Radiomobile or an HMV of various types. Control unit fitted in glovebox, power unit/amplifier and loudspeaker mounted under scuttle.

Radio aerial, fitted to the side of the scuttle.

Extra fuel pump and duplicated fuel lines (standard on Mark II, and recommended fitting if engine was to be tuned).

Wire wheel replacement service kit (ACG 5163), incorporating TF wire wheels, hubs, etc. Believed offered only after TF had been introduced, and production of the TD therefore ceased.

A range of competition and engine tuning parts were also available, for details see the section on engine tuning.

OPTIONAL EXTRAS (TF)

External mirror, or luggage carrier and mirror (as for TD).

Badge bar and fog lamp mounting.

Fog lamp (Lucas SFT576) or spot lamp (Lucas SLR576).

Andrex friction shock absorbers.

Alternative rear axle ratios, 5.125:1 (8/41) or 4.55:1 (9/41).

Full-length tonneau cover with zip, in biscuit 'imitation mohair'.

Wire wheels.

Radio and aerial (remarks as for TD).

Whitewall tyres; possibly Dunlop racing tyres.

The following heater kits were approved by MG for fitting to the TF (and at least two cars were fitted with heaters by the factory): Smith's no CHS 4532; Delaney Galley no. S.1; Key Leather Co no KLA 360.

PRODUCTION CHANGES (TD)

The number in the first column is either a chassis number, prefix TD, or an engine number, prefix XPAG/TD or XPAG/TD2. Mark II chassis and engine numbers ran in the same series as the ordinary TD model.

TD/0351   (Dec 1949)
Scuttle hoop added to chassis

TD/0501(?)   (Jan 1950)
Pierced wheels replaced solid wheels.

TD/C/1123   (May 1950)
First Mark II model.

XPAG/TD/2985   (Jul 1950)
Purolator canister type oil filter replaced Wilmot Breeden oil filter.

TD/4237   (Nov 1950)
Rubber mat on floor, driver's side (LHD cars).

TD/4251   (Nov 1950)
One-piece hub and brake drum introduced.

TD/6035   (Feb 1951)
Outer front wheel bearing grease retainer: press-on steel cap replaced felt washer type.

XPAG/TD/6482   (Feb 1951)
Modified water pump with integral seal.

XPAG/TD/7576   (Apr 1951)
Oil suction filter in sump moved to central position.

TD/7624   (May 1951)
Dip left headlamps on home market cars.

TD/8142   (Jun 1951)
Lucas control box RB106/1 with separate fuse box SF6 replaced control box RF95/2.

XPAG/TD/9008   (Jun 1951)
Exhaust rockers improved with longer bosses and bushes (inlet rockers were not changed).

XPAG/TD2/9408   (Jul 1951)
8in diameter clutch replaced 7¼in diameter clutch. New flywheel, larger bell housing and stronger clutch fork shaft. Engine number prefix changed.

XPAG/TD2/10900   (Sep 1951)
Shorter dipstick tube, new dipstick.

TD/10751 (LHD)   (Oct 1951)
TD/10779 (RHD)
New instruments (speedometer, rev counter and ammeter), rheostat switch for panel lights.

TD/11111   (Oct 1951)
Redesigned housing for inner tie rod on steering rack.

TD/12285   (Dec 1951)
Threads on wheel studs and nuts, and throughout propshaft and rear axle, changed from BSF to Unified.

TD/12419   (Dec 1951)
Spare wheel studs and nuts, threads changed from BSF to Unified.

TD/13914   (Feb 1952)
Combined oil pressure and water temperature gauge replaced the original oil pressure gauge.

XPAG/TD2/14224   (Feb 1952)
Modified oil pump, oil filter with replaceable element introduced.

XPAG/TD2/14948   (Mar 1952)
New sump in finned aluminium. Capacity increased from 9 pints (5 litres) to 10½ pints (6 litres).

XPAG/TD2/15861   (Apr 1952)
New clutch lining with improved friction.

XPAG/TD2/16482   (May 1952)
New top and third shift rail to gearbox, with snap ring, and extra support at the back.

XPAG/TD2/16978   (May 1952)
Key added to speedometer drive worm gear.

XPAG/TD3/17029   (Jun 1952)
Mark II engine prefix changed to XPAG/TD3.

XPAG/TD2/17289   (Jun 1952)
Shorter pushrods with longer adjusting screws.

TD/17548   (Jun 1952)
High beam warning lamp added to speedometer.

XPAG/TD2/17969   (Jun 1952)
New cylinder block with round water passage holes, new cylinder head gasket.

XPAG/TD2/18291   (Jul 1952)
Improved material specification for exhaust valves.

TD/18883   (Aug 1952)
Foot-operated dip switch and new horn push replaced the combined horn push and dip switch.

TD/20374 (LHD)   (Sep 1952)
TD/20696 (RHD)   (Oct 1952)
Three-bow hood frame replaced two-bow hood frame; sidescreens revised to suit.

XPAG/TD2/20942   (Oct 1952)
Cotter bolt fixing for distributor introduced; no change to the distributor itself.

XPAG/TD2/20972   (Oct 1952)
New oil pump end plate incorporating priming plug.

TD/20749   (Oct 1952)
Additional body mounting point each side of chassis.

TD/21303   (Oct 1952)
Round rear lamps replaced triangular type, and rear wings modified to suit.

TD/22251   (Nov 1952)
XPAG/TD/22717
Rod operated clutch linkage replaced cable operation, and clutch stop bolt added.

TD/22315   (Nov 1952)
Flashing direction indicators fitted on cars to North American specification. Wiper motor moved to centre of the windscreen frame.

TD/22407   (Nov 1952)
Floorboards changed.

XPAG/TD2/22735   (Nov 1952)
Cylinder head with round water passage holes, and new cylinder head gasket. L10S plugs (¾in reach) replaced NA8 plugs (½in reach).

TD/C/22613   (Dec 1952)
Special trim package for Mark II model; compression ratio on Mark II engines lowered.

XPAG/TD2/24116   (Jan 1953)
New camshaft, as used subsequently on TF. Revised valve timing, improved torque at lower revs. Tappet clearance altered from .019in to .012in, and new tappet clearance plate to rocker cover.

XPAG/TD2/24489   (Jan 1953)
New type of oil suction filter. Points gap clearance changed from .010/.012in to .014/.016in.

TD/25973   (Mar 1953)
New type of tie rod outer ends with improved seals.

XPAG/TD2/26635   (Mar 1953)
New type of oil pump body.

XPAG/TD2/27551   (Apr 1953)
Improved material specification for crankshaft.

XPAG/TD2/27867   (May 1953)
Height of valve spring faces reduced, valve guides slightly more protruding.

XPAG/TD2/28167   (May 1953)
Holes drilled for locking wire in heads of bolts for rocker shaft supports.

PRODUCTION CHANGES (TF)

The fairly extensive changes made from the TD to the TF at the start of TF production are detailed in the body of the text. Therefore only modifications made during the TF production run are listed here, with as usual a chassis number (prefix TF) or an engine number (prefix XPAG/TF, or XPEG) in the first column. TF 1500 chassis numbers continued in the TF series, but there was a new series of engine numbers for the XPEG engine.

TF/1501   (Dec 1953)
XPAG/TF/31537
Low-pressure fuel pump (SU L-type AUA 25) mounted under bonnet replaced by high-pressure pump (SU HP-type, AUA 57) mounted on chassis side member in front of right-hand rear wheel arch. Wiring loom altered to suit.

XPAG/TF/31263   (Dec 1953)
Oil pump modified with hole drilled in priming plug, to make pump self-priming.

XPAG/TF/31857   (Dec 1953)
Modified ignition high-tension cables.

XPAG/TF/31943   (Dec 1953)
Reduced internal diameter to lower banjo oil coupling on oil pipe from oil gallery to cylinder head.

XPAG/TF/33024   (Feb 1954)
Modified oil suction pipe and sump.

TF/3495   (Feb 1954)
Piston dampers added to carburettor dashpots.

TF/3811   (Apr 1954)
Improved front wheel grease retainers on cars fitted with wire wheels.

TF/4760   (Apr 1954)
Threads on tie rod and ball studs, and on tie rod greasers, changed from BSF to Unified.

TF/6501   (Jul 1954)
(XPEG/501)
First TF 1500 car with 1466cc engine. TF 1500 badges added to bonnet sides, and reflectors to rear of car (new legal requirement in the UK).

TF/6887   (Aug 1954)
Wire wheels with deeper dished inner flange.

TF/6950   (Sep 1954)
Last TF with 1250cc XPAG/TF engine.

TF/8146   (Nov 1954)
New casting for body of horns; the horns were still known to Lucas as type WT618.

PRODUCTION AND EXPORT FIGURES (TD)

There were 29,664 production TDs (compare previous section), of which at least 1710 cars were Mark II models (see Mark II section). The following statistics were kept by the Production Control Department in the Abingdon factory:

	1949	1950	1951	1952	1953	Total, all years
Home market	2	149	385	246	874	1656
Export, RHD	96	1268	940	371	280	2955
Export, LHD	0	142	292	285	237	956
Export, North America	0	2810	5756	9901	5021	23488
Chassis only, RHD	0	4	0	2	3	9
Chassis only, LHD	0	6	48	13	90	157
CKD cars, RHD	0	388	30	20	5	443
All specifications	**98**	**4767**	**7451**	**10838**	**6510**	**29664**

Of the 103 LHD chassis in 1952-53, 100 were for Bertone-bodied Arnolt-MGs (the provenance of the chassis for the original show cars is not easily established). CKD cars were exported to South Africa (345 cars) and Eire (98 cars).

The following were the major export markets, according to Nuffield Exports:

	1949	1950	1951	1952	1953	Total, all years
USA (of which Mark II)	6	2495	4988 (467)	9009 (959)	3509 (129)	20007 (1555)
West Germany	0	124	126	345	653	1248
Canada	2	233	358	170	383	1146
Australia	8	292	405	87	112	904
Belgium	0	218	164	46	73	501
Switzerland	0	219	134	44	27	424
France	0	16	17	94	223	350
South Africa (of which CKD)	0	331 (330)	15 (15)	1	0	347 (345)
Japan	0	14	191	51	30	286
Malaya	3	28	38	54	58	181
Brazil	0	6	0	143	0	149
Rhodesia	3	25	86	15	17	146
Sweden	0	44	27	42	18	131
The Netherlands	0	33	70	9	15	127
Venezuela	0	11	22	36	45	114
Eire (of which CKD)	0	45 (43)	30 (30)	20 (20)	5 (5)	100 (98)
Total of above	**22**	**4134**	**6671**	**10166**	**5168**	**26161**
Total of all exports (of which Mark II)	**30**	**4431**	**7084** (480)	**10936** (976)	**5823** (212)	**28007** (1668)

PRODUCTION AND EXPORT FIGURES (TF)

Of the 9600 production TFs, there were 6200 TF 1250s and 3400 TF 1500s. The following statistics have been compiled by the author by going through the actual production record ledger. It reveals that there were rather fewer home market TFs than has previously been thought, and it also gives the precise split between TF 1250 and TF 1500 models to each specification:

	1953 TF 1250	1954 TF 1250	1954 TF 1500	1955 TF 1500	Total, all years TF 1250 and TF 1500	
Home market	77	736	47	197	1057	
Export, RHD	123	1084	19	503	1729	
Export, LHD	61	359	24	48	492	
Export, North America	1374	2374★	1826	661	6235	★incl. 2 RHD cars
Chassis only, RHD	0	2	0	0	2	(for home market)
CKD cars, RHD	0	10	0	0	10	(for Eire)
CKD cars, LHD	0	0	35	40	75	(for Mexico)
All specifications	**1635**	**4565**	**1951**	**1449**	**9600**	

The following were the major export markets, according to Nuffield Exports; unfortunately the export figures for 1955 are not available.

	1953 TF 1250	1954 TF 1250	1954 TF 1500	Total, TF 1250 and TF 1500	1953–54
USA	611	1614	1506	3731	
Australia	20	793	0	813	
West Germany	226	393	85	704	
Canada	12	262	0	274	
France	46	125	7	178	
Switzerland	16	62	5	83	
Belgium	5	70	0	75	
Mexico	0	60	15★	75	★CKD cars
Sweden	13	60	0	73	
Italy	1	62	0	63	
Venezuela	20	40	0	60	
Rhodesia	5	54	0	59	
New Zealand	0	53	0	53	
(French) Morocco	3	44	0	47	
Malaya	0	46	0	46	
Japan	17	26	0	43	
Total of above	**995**	**3764**	**1618**	**6377**	
Total of all exports	**1114**	**4275**	**1643**	**7032**	

COLOUR SCHEMES (TD & TF)

When the TD was launched, it was offered in the same range of colour schemes which had been available on the final TCs, as follows:

    Black, with Red, Beige or Green trim
    MG Red, with Red or Beige trim
    Almond Green, with Beige trim (Green trim optional on 1951 models)
    Ivory, with Red or Green trim
    Clipper Blue, with Beige trim

Some TDs finished in Almond Green had metallic paint on the body and matching solid green paint on the wings and valances (as had been the case with the pre-war Metallic Grey colour on the TA and TB models).

In late 1950, the following two additional colours became available on the TD:

    Autumn Red, with Red or Beige trim
    Sun Bronze (metallic), with Red or Green trim

Autumn Red was a much darker colour than the bright MG Red.

The range of seven paint colours lasted only through the 1951 model year, and for 1952 and 1953 the TD was offered in the following colours:

    Black, with Red or Green trim
    MG Red, with Red trim
    Woodland Green, with Green trim
    Ivory, with Red or Green trim
    Silver Streak Grey (metallic), with Red trim

Woodland Green was a darker green colour than Almond or MG Green. In 1953, Beige trim was re-introduced as an option on cars in Black, MG Red and Woodland Green, but only on home market specification cars.

The TF was available in the following colour schemes throughout the production run from 1953 to 1955, with no changes:

    Black, with Red, Green or Biscuit trim
    MG Red, with Red or Biscuit trim
    Almond Green (or MG Green), with Green or Biscuit trim
    Ivory, with Red or Green trim
    Birch Grey, with Red trim

Some TFs were finished in metallic Almond (or MG) Green. An American correspondent has stated that he believes some TFs were finished in the darker Autumn Red rather than MG Red; well, it is not impossible...

On both the TD and TF, the colours for other components followed the pattern set with the TC: hoods and sidescreens in biscuit; carpets in black; tonneau cover normally in biscuit but possibly in black; and wheels, whether disc or wire, in silver. On the TD, the radiator slats were painted to match the upholstery (but see remarks in the TC colour list and in the section on the TD cooling system), the exception being late Mark II cars with chromed-plated slats, also found on all TFs.

Cellulose (lacquer) paint continued to be used on the TD. TFs were finished in a combination of cellulose paint on the body and synthetic (enamel) paint on the wings and valances. The reason for this was probably that synthetic paint had greater resistance to chipping. However, green TFs were finished entirely in cellulose; there may have been problems getting an exact colour match with the two different types of paint in green, particularly when metallic green was used. The underside of the wings was finished in body colour.

The only T Series model for which records are preserved showing the colours of inidividual cars is the TF. I have gone through the TF records to establish how many cars were painted in the five different colours and have come up with the following figures: Red, 3190 cars (33%); Black, 1881 cars (20%); Ivory, 1712 cars (18%); Green, 1521 cars (16%); Grey, 1207 cars (12%). The eagle-eyed reader will immediately have spotted that there are 89 cars (1%) unaccounted for. Of these, 85 were the CKD cars; two were delivered in the chassis-only form; and two were special colour orders, of which one was delivered in Primer (with Red trim), and one car was actually finished from the factory in White with Black trim. There may equally well have been a few special colour orders among the TDs – although I am inclined to think that contemporary pictures of two-tone TDs in the USA were the results of quick on-the-spot re-sprays by local dealers before delivery to customers.

Most post-war colours are still recognised by paint manufacturers, and the following table lists the colour code numbers such as they are available from ICI in the UK, or from Ditzler and Rinshed-Mason in the USA:

MG colour name	ICI code	Ditzler code	Rinshed-Mason code
Clipper Blue	not known	12297	BM 042
Sequoia Cream/Ivory	4138 or 2700?	80203	BM 127
MG/Almond Green	2007 (metallic)	44159	BM 076
Woodland Green	0191	2246	BM 078
Silver Streak Grey	2209	72030	n/a
Birch Grey	2507	31918	BM 002
MG Red	9448	71993	BM 121 R
Autumn Red	2752	50930	BM 108 R
Sun Bronze	2027	23662	n/a

However, I am not totally happy that Sequoia Cream and Ivory are the same colour, nor MG Green and Almond Green – and I am not convinced that the TC colour Shires Green is the same as either MG or Almond Green. Neither does this table distinguish between metallic and non-metallic MG and Almond Green.

Buying Guide

There is usually a good selection of T-types available on the market at any given time. In Britain, the TC is likely to be most common, but there is a growing number of TDs and TFs, and quite a few TAs, but the TB is understandably a rarity. In the USA, the TD predominates, the TC and the TF are relatively common, and pre-war models are very scarce. In other countries the numbers of preserved cars are much smaller, and most are post-war models.

In the 1980s there has been a growing tendency for classic cars of the commercially marketable kind (and any T-type is certainly that) to change hands through dealers. This applies especially in those now frequent cases where a car is sold from one country to another. They used to be shipped out of Britain, either to the USA or to Europe, but with ups and downs in the exchange rate the flow is now coming back across the Atlantic. Many cars from the USA are finding new homes in Britain, in Europe – convenient because American TDs and TFs have left-hand drive – and even in Australia.

With T-types ranging in age from almost 35 years for the youngest TF to more than 50 for the oldest TA, it would be too much to expect to find the well-maintained low-mileage all-original one owner car. Apart from that, few T-types were owned by little old ladies (although some may have been by vicars!) from new. Any car now coming on the market is likely to have had some restoration work carried out at some stage. A few cars still seem to turn up in unrestored condition, which is a nice way of saying that they are wrecks.

The most important things to look for are a sound chassis – not rusted, nor bent, nor cracked – and an engine which can be rebuilt. If a running engine shows less than 40psi oil pressure when hot, a rebuild is likely to be needed. Almost anything else is available from the T-type spares suppliers. Complete new bodies are available, and virtually any other part can be bought, renovated or remanufactured. There is not actually an acute shortage of engines except for the not very robust MPJG engines fitted originally to the TA models (many of which have been fitted with XPAG engines from later cars). However, some specialists are now buying engines from the Wolseley 4/44 saloon, which used a single-carburettor version of the TD/TF engine, and of

which 30,000 were made from 1953 to 1956. The cylinder block and crankshaft from these can, with a few modifications, be worked into rebuilt XP-engines to MG specification.

Any T-type is extremely simple in design and construction. I do not mean that they are crude or unsophisticated – they were in fact very well made – but in common with most MGs built at Abingdon they were largely assembled cars, made up of components and sub-assemblies from many sources, and put together in frankly primitive conditions. Therefore, the cars had to be simple; and, to be honest, they were always built to a price. But this all works to the advantage of the present-day owner or restorer of a T-type; I can think of no other classic sports car which is as suitable for the enthusiastic amateur restorer working in the garage at home. And because of steadily increasing values, a T-type MG is now a car which at the end of a restoration project may be worth the time and money that has been spent.

For those enthusiasts who simply want to enjoy the car without having to worry about restoring it, there are perfectly useable cars available. And if work is needed, there are MG specialists or general classic car restorers prepared to undertake it. If possible, try to shop around, or get recommendations from fellow club members.

Not very many T-type owners are now likely to rely solely on the car for their everyday motoring needs – a T-type is for high days and holidays. For limited usage, there is not a great deal to choose between different models. You would not expect to be able to compete with modern cars on performance – the quickest T-type, the TF 1500, has a top speed of 85-88mph, and will get from 0 to 60mph in just over 16sec – but you will be able to keep up with most traffic. The cars steer and brake well enough by modern standards, and your fuel consumption should be well on the right side of 30mpg (9 litres per 100 km). From the useability point of view, the TD and TF probably have the edge, with more comfortable suspension and roomier cockpits.

It would be a futile exercise to try to quote actual values, but it may be pointed out that through the 1980s a good T-type has virtually doubled in value. Of the different models, it seems that a TF, particularly a TF 1500, is worth anything up to 50 per cent more than a TC or TD.

Clubs and Specialists

The MG Car Club
Kimber House
12 Cemetery Road
Abingdon
Oxfordshire OX14 1FF

Originally established by the MG company in 1930, for the past 20 years this has been an independent club. It offers a wide variety of sporting and social events, and runs individual registers for all models of MG. There are many local centres in the UK, and local centres or affiliated clubs world-wide. The club publishes a monthly magazine, Safety Fast, *and many of the registers have their own publications as well. Club president; John Thornley OBE. Chairman: Will Corry. Administrator: Lyn Jeffrey.*

The MG Owners Club
2/4 Station Road
Swavesey
Cambs CB4 5QZ
Tel: 0954 31125

Formed in 1973, this has grown to be the largest one-make car club in the world, with 50,000 members. The club has well-supported local groups throughout the UK, and offers an attractive range of facilities, including technical advice, a club shop, an insurance scheme and a monthly colour magazine, Enjoying MG, *as well as a yearbook. A range of reprinted technical literature is available, and the club runs an approval scheme for MG specialist restorers and parts suppliers, as well as its own workshop at Swavesey. Club secretary: Roche Bentley.*

The Octagon Car Club
36 Queensville Avenue
Stafford ST17 4LS
Tel: 0785 51014

Run by enthusiasts for enthusiasts, this is a smaller but rapidly-expanding club which is unique in the UK in catering solely for the pre-1956 MGs, including all the T Series models. A monthly 'Bulletin' is published. The club offers technical information, and a spares and book service. Regional meetings are held in many parts of the country. This club organises the annual 'Wings' run, a pilgrimage to Abingdon. Club secretary: Harry Crutchley.

The New England MG T Register Ltd
Drawer 220
Oneonta
NY 13820
USA

The main club for T Series (and other pre-1956) MGs in North America, dedicated to the maintenance, preservation and enjoyment of these cars. Publishes an excellent bi-monthly magazine, Sacred Octagon, *as well as other publications such as* The T-Series Handbook. *Organises two major rallies each year, the 'Gatherings of the Faithful', at various locations in North-Eastern USA, as well as other local and national events. Numerous affiliated local clubs and chapters throughout the USA. Club secretary and editor: Dick Knudson.*

There are also two specialist magazines covering MG cars which will be of interest to T Series owners and enthusiasts:

MG Enthusiast Magazine
PO Box 11
Dewsbury
W. Yorks WF12 7UZ
Editor: Martyn Wise

MG Magazine
PO Box 321
Otego
NY 13825
USA
Editor: Ron Embling

SPECIALISTS

The following information is believed to be correct as of early 1989. Neither the author nor the publishers will be held liable for any errors or omissions or the consequences thereof. No recommendation is implied by the inclusion of a firm in this section.

UK

Barry M. Bone, 'Quoins', Jarvis Lane, Steyning, Sussex. Tel: 0903 813355
Parts, cars for sale

Anthony Brier, 6A Far End Lane, Honley, Huddersfield, West Yorkshire HD7 2NS. Tel: 0484 664669
Parts, service and repairs, restoration

Brown & Gammons, r/o 18 High Street, Baldock, Hertfordshire SG7 6AS. Tel: 0462 893914
Parts, restoration and service

W. M. Collingburn, Kimber House, Lombard's Wynd, Richmond, N. Yorks DL10 4JY. Tel: 0748 4105
Coachtrimmer, complete interiors for T Series cars

S. J. Gilbert, 33 Pyrcroft Lane, Weybridge, Surrey KT13 9XP. Tel: 0932 43712
Manufacturer of body panels

Kimble Engineering, 33 Highfield Road, Birmingham B28 OEV. Tel: 021 777 2011
Manufacturer of parts

Moss Spares (UK) Ltd, 15 Allington Way, Yarm Road Industrial Estate, Darlington DL1 4QB. Tel: 0325 281343
Parts

Moto-Build Ltd, 328 Bath Road, West Hounslow, Middlesex. Tel: 01 572 5437
Parts, restoration, car sales: including stocks from well-known Toulmin firm

Naylor Brothers, Airedale Garage, Hollins Hill, Shipley, W. Yorks BD17 7QN. Tel: 0274 585161
Restoration: the original maker of the Naylor TF 1700

Naylor Brothers MG Parts Ltd, Regent House, Dockfield Road, Shipley, W. Yorks BD17 7SF. Tel: 0274 594071
Parts

North-West MG Centre, Green Farm, Duke Street, Holme via Carnforth, Lancashire LA6 1PY. Tel: 0524 781377
Parts

NTG Motor Services Ltd, 282-284 Bramford Road, Ipswich, Suffolk. Tel: 0473 211240
Parts; also MG Y-type specialists

Octagon Cars Ltd, The Craft Centre, Chart Sutton, Maidstone, Kent ME17 3RX. Tel: 0622 843445
Parts; wire wheel specialists

The Pre-War MG Parts Centre, 1A Albany Road, Chislehurst, Kent BR7 6BG. Tel: 01 467 7788
Parts (mostly TA-TC, and for pre-1936 MGs), cars for sale

Ray Sales, PO Box 73, Bracknell, Berkshire. Tel: 0344 483070 *Manufacturer of parts*

Sports and Vintage Motors Ltd, Upper Battlefield, Shrewsbury SY4 3DB. Tel: 09397 458
Parts (mostly TA-TC, and for pre-1936 MGs)

Vintage Restorations, The Old Bakery, Windmill Street, Tunbridge Wells, Kent TN2 4UU. Tel: 0892 25899
Restoration of instruments

USA

Abingdon Classics, 12 Old Redding Road, W. Redding, CT 06896. Tel: 203 438 6865
Restoration

Abingdon Spares Ltd, PO Box 37 (OB), South Street, Walpole, NH 03608. Tel: 603 756 4768; toll-free order phone 800-225-0251
Parts (the proprietor, Gerry Goguen, owns and runs the MG Museum in nearby Westminster, Vermont; the largest MG collection in the world open to the public)

Jim Bigler, 496 North Coast Highway, Laguna Beach, CA 92561. Tel: 714 497 2221
Restoration, second hand parts

British Automotive Ltd, 579 Garfield Street, Eugene, OR 97402. Tel: 503 484 2043
Parts and repairs

M & G Vintage Auto, 265 Rte #71, Tuxedo Park, NY 10987. Tel: 914 753 5900; toll-free 800-631-8990
Parts, service and restoration

Moss Motors Ltd, PO Box MG, 7200 Hollister Avenue, Goleta, CA 93116. Tel: 805 968 1041; toll-free 800-322-6985 (in CA) or 800- 235-6954
Parts

Motor Good, 809 Heavenly Lane, Cincinnati, OH 45238. Tel: 513 922 8076
Parts

Motorhead Ltd, 3221 Wilson Boulevard, Arlington, VA 22201. Tel: 703 527 3140
General MG parts supplier

O'Connor Classic Autos, 2569 Scott Boulevard, Santa Clara, CA 95050. Tel: 408 727 0430
Parts for TC to TF

University Motors (USA) Ltd, 614–G Eastern Avenue SE, Grand Rapids, MI 49503. Tel: 616 245 2141
Parts, restoration, technical advice for TD and TF

Whitworth Shop, 14444 Watt Road, Novelty, OH 44072. Tel: 216 338 5950
Parts, restoration

Parts suppliers in other parts of the world

MG Sales & Service, 197 Torrens Road, Ridleyton, SA 5007, Australia.
Stevens-MG Ersatzteile, Oststrasse 29-31, 4230 Wesel, W. Germany.
Triple M Garage, 3044 Delmsen 4, W. Germany.
C & C Parts, Hei 1, 5991 PC Baarlo, The Netherlands.
Damen en Kroes B.v., Lindendijk 2-4, PO Box 32, 5490 AA Sint-Oedenrode, The Netherlands.
Octagon Spares b.v., Burg van Niekerklaan 19, 2182 GK Hillegom, The Netherlands.
Advanced Parts & Spares Ltd, 11 Honan Place, Avondale, Auckland, New Zealand.
MG Centre Sweden, Verkstadsgatan 4, Kungsbakca, Sweden.
Minelli Corporation, Mattenstrasse 3, 8330 Pfaffikon/ZH, Switzerland.

This list is by no means exhaustive but it is hoped it gives a good cross-section of T Series specialists. Many other firms, particularly in the UK and the USA, offer parts and restoration services for the T-types. Reference to other specialists will often be found in club publications or specialist magazines.